RELEASING THE BOUNDS OF SHAME

RELEASING THE BOUNDS OF SHAME

My Recovery from Mental Illness and Cybersex Addiction

Robert Gray

MOUNTAIN ARBOR
PRESS

Alpharetta, GA

This ISBN is the property of Mountain Arbor Press for the express purpose of sales and distribution of this title. The content of this book is the property of the copyright holder only. BookLogix does not hold any ownership of the content of this book and is not liable in any way for the materials contained within. The views and opinions expressed in this book are the property of the author, and do not necessarily reflect those of Mountain Arbor Press.

Some names and identifying details have been changed to protect the privacy of individuals.

The author has tried to recreate events, locations, and conversations from his memories of them. In some instances, in order to maintain their anonymity, the author has changed the names of individuals and places. He may also have changed some identifying characteristics and details such as physical attributes, occupations, and places of residence.

Copyright © 2020 by Robert Gray

All rights reserved. No part of this book may be reproduced or transmitted in any form or by any means, electronic or mechanical, including photocopying, recording, or any information storage and retrieval system, without permission in writing from the author.

ISBN: 978-1-63183-844-6 - Paperback
eISBN: 978-1-63183-845-3 - ePub
eISBN: 978-1-63183-846-0 - mobi

Printed in the United States of America   0 5 2 2 2 0

⊗This paper meets the requirements of ANSI/NISO Z39.48-1992 (Permanence of Paper)

Scripture and translation from Siddur Lev Shalem Rabbinical Assembly (2016).

This book is dedicated to my beloved wife, Lauren, who has always been my rock, even when I was at rock bottom.

בָּרוּךְ אַתָּה ה' אֱלֹהֵינוּ מֶלֶךְ
הָעוֹלָם. מַתִּיר אֲסוּרִים.

Blessed be the Lord our God and king of the world, who releases the bound.

"Owning our story can be hard but not nearly as difficult as spending our lives running from it. Embracing our vulnerabilities is risky but not nearly as dangerous as giving up on love and belonging and joy—the experiences that make us the most vulnerable. Only when we are brave enough to explore the darkness will we discover the infinite power of our light."

—Brené Brown
Research Professor, University of Houston

Contents

Note to the Reader

In my attempt to "connect the dots" from my childhood to make sense of my eventual struggles with mental illness and addiction, you may reach the conclusion that I blame my parents. Please understand that I have always loved my mother and father and have nothing more than the utmost respect for them. They survived one of the most horrible times in human history, left their homeland to come to America, and raised a family. They did the best they could with what they had at the time. I am forever grateful for the life they provided me. May they rest in peace.

Introduction

Each year at our Passover Seder, I would ask the *Ma Nishtanah* (The Four Questions) from our Haggadah. Since I was the youngest in the family, the honor fell to me. I would sing the questions as I had learned them in Hebrew school, and then my father would provide the answers. He did this exclusively in Hebrew, at a very fast pace, and with an old Ashkenazic style of pronunciation, so I didn't pay a lot of attention. My main concern was how long would it be until we could finally eat our Passover meal. When I had a family of my own and I was the leader of the Seder, we usually took turns reading from the Haggadah in English. This is how most of our friends conducted their Seders so that they would be more meaningful and understandable. Plus, not many of us could *daven* (pray) in Hebrew the way my dad could.

The answer to The Four Questions contains passages from the Torah about The Four Sons. The Torah describes four children who ask questions about the Exodus. Tradition teaches that these verses refer to four different types of children. The wise child asks a very detailed and lengthy question, "What are the testimonies, the statutes, and the ordinances, which the Lord our God has commanded you?" (Deuteronomy 6:20–23). The wicked child asks a question with some amount of sarcasm, "What does this Passover service mean to *you*?" (Exodus 12:26–27). The simple child asks a very uncomplicated question, "What is this?" (Exodus 13:14). And then there is a child who does not know to ask—Exodus 13:8. With this child, the parent must initiate the conversation and provide the answer to the unasked question.

I believe that there is a fifth type of child. This child may be wise, wicked, or simple. And he knows how to ask a question. In fact, he has many questions about himself and his environment. He often wonders if other children ever feel the way he does, but he doubts that they do. He assumes that other children think poorly of him and wouldn't want to be his friend. This child thinks that other children are happier, more popular, more confident, and less afraid. This child thinks that he is just different. He is painfully shy. He wants to fit in. He is afraid to make mistakes. He is afraid to admit that he did something wrong. He is terrified to admit that he doesn't know something or can't do something. Anything he does is just never good enough. He feels alone because no one else could be like this. No one else could understand. He can't talk about his feelings with other children because they would tease him or make fun of him. He can't talk about his feelings to teachers or other adults because he can't let anyone know that he is different. He can't ask for help. He must suffer in silence and conceal his feelings of inadequacy. He hides behind his mask, which is his sense of humor. He jokes, he laughs, he appears to be happy. But he can't let anyone get under the mask. He can't let them see his feelings of pain. He feels so alone. He can't cry out for help. He can't let them see he is flawed. He is not one of The Four Children. He is the fifth child: the child who is afraid to ask.

I am The Fifth Child. I lived in a nice neighborhood and was educated in one of the best school systems in the area. I was a talented musician and earned the opportunity to play in one of the best university marching bands in the country. I was one of the smartest students in my classes, and I succeeded in earning an undergraduate degree and two graduate degrees. I got married and, with my amazing wife, succeeded in raising four children (including triplets) who are all now happily married. I was employed by several corporations as well as a nonprofit organization for which I continue to do volunteer work. I am now happily retired and collecting social security. I guess most people would say I am living a wonderful life. And I am. I have so many things for which I am grateful. But all of my fears and insecurities stayed behind my mask, hidden as deep, dark secrets. I kept my fears to myself. I suffered in silence. I gutted it out.

Since I never asked for help, I am quite certain that I was living with clinical depression for many years. In my forties, I discovered the attraction to the internet and developed some addictive behaviors which led me to make many horrible deci-sions. After several years of keeping secrets and living a life of hell, I finally reached a point where I had to ask for help. My depression became se-vere, and I became suicidal. Two things saved my life: the undying love from my family and electro-convulsive therapy.

Yes, I have much to be grateful for. But I wonder how life would have turned out if The Fifth Child could have spoken up years ago.

Prologue

Before I finally sat down to start writing this book, it had been on my mind for many years. In fact, this is not the first book that I thought I would write. Back in the 1980s, my wife Lauren and I struggled with infertility. In 1982, before knowing we were going to have problems, Lauren had an ectopic pregnancy which didn't last more than a few weeks. For most of the remainder of the decade, we had to deal with medications, tests, surgery, specialists, and the antiseptic, unfeeling world of medicine. It was an emotionally trying time for both of us and, after it was over and we were blessed with four children, I wanted to write a book about our experiences. It was going to be called *The Job of Infertility* and would focus on the effects the process had on our relationship and how little was done to support us as people through our struggle. We were on our own in terms of dealing with our emotions of guilt and our feelings of inadequacy. Infertility is nobody's fault, but I felt responsible for not being enough of a man to create a child. Each time one of our friends joyfully announced a baby on the way, it was a blow to our self-esteem. If there was support for people like us, we sure didn't know about it, and none of our doctors ever mentioned it. Perhaps we should have asked, but I think we were too ashamed to let anyone know that we were struggling. The book was taking shape in my mind, but I had no idea how to write a book and get it published. Through my involvement in a group called New Warriors, I was friends with a writer for *Playboy* Magazine. He wrote many articles for and about men, and I met him in one of our support group meetings. I wrote him a letter in which I described my desire to write my book. He responded with suggestions about starting out writing articles for magazines and working my way up to a book since a book would be quite a challenge. I told him that I could picture the book in my mind and that it was my dream to write it. He told me to follow my dream and go for it. The book remained my dream. I never wrote a single word of it. I thought that it would be a failure. I believed that nobody would buy it or be interested in my story. I never was a good writer, so why did I think that I could actually write a book? These were just some of the many negative thoughts and ideas going through my mind.

The fact that you are now holding and reading this book means that I have managed to overcome the same beliefs and fears about this book. I have thought about writing this book for many years. My online friends were probably getting sick and tired of hearing about it for all these years. And yet, the fear of failure, the believed inadequacy in my writing ability, and the thought that my illness was not "bad" enough all held me back. Who would want to read my story? After all, it is just a story about basic depression. I was never strung out on drugs, never homeless, never in prison. I wasn't sick enough to write a story. In my mind, even my depression wasn't good enough.

After becoming a Certified Peer Specialist and working for the Georgia Mental Health Consumer Network, I learned how important it was to tell my story. The greatest gift I can give someone who is battling the effects of a mental health challenge is hope. When I was lying in my bed alone, day after day, week after week, hope disappeared. As the level of hope dwindled, the level of desperation increased. My bedroom became my prison cell and, although the door was open and I could escape at will, I remained imprisoned. I was unaware of support groups and I knew of no one whom I could turn to who could understand my plight. As a Certified Peer Specialist, I supported people every day who were losing or had lost hope. Their stories didn't matter to me. There was no such thing as a "bad" enough story. The only thing that mattered was that I could understand and empathize. Sometimes, I had to hold the hope for people until they were able to hold it for themselves. So, to all of you who are reading this book, no matter how many of you there are, I wrote this book for you to support you in finding, grasping, and holding on to your hope. Most of all, I wrote this book to encourage you to ask for support. Get out from behind your mask of secrecy. It is not protecting you. It is

preventing you from healing. And to all of you who
are caregivers of loved ones who are struggling, just
know that you are their standing stone.

Chapter One
How Did I Get Here?

It's the middle of the night in mid-July in 1998. For the past few years, I have been living a secret life on the internet. I was involved in clandestine relationships with women in cyberspace. I was addicted to cybersex and the fantasy world which the internet provided me every day. My addiction to these relationships led me to risk my family and my career for the excitement of this secret life of internet infidelity. I tried to stop several times but, as with many addictions, I was drawn back each time until I crashed. The crash occurred when my fantasy life became real, when online and phone sex weren't satisfying enough for me. I crossed the line I never thought I would cross. I met a woman in person. After that I stayed in my bed, surrounded by the deep darkness of depression. I felt the enormous weight of the darkness that separated me from my family and friends.

Lauren drove me to a psychiatric hospital. This was my second visit to a hospital and it provided me my final option. I was facing the prospect of electroconvulsive therapy (ECT) and I was scared to death. Would I go through with it? Would I allow it? Could I be forced into having the treatment? What would happen to me if it didn't work?

How did I ever get here? What was so bad about my life that events led me to this? After all, I was raised in a pretty nice suburban area of Detroit. I was a great student in school. I was accepted into my dream school, the University of Michigan, where I enjoyed my time in the marching band, majored in psychology, and met the love of my life. I continued my education to earn an MBA, got married while in graduate school, and landed a managerial position with a telephone company in my hometown of Detroit. I was enjoying my twentieth year with the telephone company and celebrated our twentieth wedding anniversary. We were blessed with four children, our fourteen-year-old daughter Aline, whose Bat Mitzvah we celebrated the year before, and our nine-year-old triplets Hilary, Michael, and Eric. We were seemingly living the American Dream with a mortgage, car payments, and too much debt. I couldn't ask for more. And yet, for the past few years, I was hiding my emotional struggles and behaviors that enabled me to avoid my problems and stress. For the past several months, I remained isolated in the perceived safety of my room and my bed. I stopped going to work. I ignored my family and friends. Rumination and panic attacks took over, leaving me a willing prisoner of my own despair. Here I was, the poster boy for a wonderful life, on my way for a treatment considered barbaric and inhumane by some. I had fought against ECT because I was so afraid of what I would be like when it was over. I couldn't believe that my situation had gotten to this point. But we had tried talk therapy and medication to no avail. I was afraid to even think about what would happen if this didn't work. What was left for me? Lobotomy? Life in an institution in a medically induced stupor? My own real-life version of *One Flew Over the Cuckoo's Nest*. I was forty-four years old and had so much to live for. If only I could convince myself of that. Tomorrow morning the electrodes would be placed on my head, the current would run through my brain causing a seizure, my body would twitch, and, a short time later, I would awaken in the recovery room. Unless something went wrong and I died on the table. What would I feel when I awoke? Would it all be the same or even worse? Would I remember anything, or would my mind be some kind of a blank slate? Or would I miraculously find myself in a better frame of mind? Was I fated to live a life in complete and utter darkness and hopelessness? Or would I be bathed in the light of hope and recovery? I had no idea and I was terrified, but ECT was my last hope.

Chapter Two
In the Beginning

April 9, 1954. It was a day like many others in Detroit. The high temperature was forty-eight degrees Fahrenheit with a low of thirty degrees. There was a southeasterly wind and no rain or snow that day. It had been warmer during the week, as it would be the following week. I was born into this world on a cold day. Figures.

At birth, I was a five-pound-four-ounce bundle of joy. My brother was born in 1946, and I was my mother's last child. She really wanted a girl. When she was told that her last child was another boy, she didn't want to hold me. Of course, I have no memory of my first encounter with my mother. But I remember her telling me that she said, "Take him away." She didn't want to see me. And so, my story begins with an early rejection.

Because I was such a small baby, I was given an ironic nickname. In Hungarian, it was spelled Csabi and was pronounced almost exactly like Chubby. During my elementary school years, I grew into that name and was overweight for much of my childhood. Some of my cousins used to tease me because of my nickname and appearance and would call me fat. I hated that, and I would tell them that I was well built. But I felt the shame and ridicule in school as well, and I became very self-conscious about my appearance. The main reason why I never learned to swim was because of my weight. I hated taking off my shirt, and I felt self-conscious about wearing a T-shirt in the water. My mom wanted me to take swimming lessons, but I never did. It was just too embarrassing, and I didn't want to be teased. In addition to having a large stomach, my chest looked like I was developing boobs. I really despised having to play shirts against skins basketball in gym class.

My parents, Imre Goldstein and Klára Ehrenfeld, were Hungarian Jews who survived the Holocaust. They came to the United States in 1949 with their two-and-a-half-year-old son and all their belongings to start a new life. Their ship landed in Boston and my parents ventured to Iowa, where one of my mother's sisters lived. She had married a non-Jewish American and settled in his hometown in Council Bluffs. His family did not know that his wife (my aunt) was Jewish, so, when my parents lived there, they had to keep the secret as well. With a name like Goldstein, it was rather obvious that they were Jews. So, they used an alias last name of Garay, which was a common Hungarian name. They began their life in a new land, learned a new language, and tried to put their horrific past behind them. My father was trained as an automobile mechanic, and one of his relatives worked for a large automobile manufacturer in Detroit. He suggested that my father could find work in the automobile assembly plants there, prompting them to settle in Detroit, where I was born a few years later.

I was a rambunctious child. I caused a lot of trouble and did a lot of things that I shouldn't have done. Perhaps I was seeking attention and trying to be noticed. Maybe I felt that my brother got all of the attention and I needed some of my own. I really don't know and can't remember my motivations. As an adult looking back, I would say that I needed a good dose of discipline. But I didn't get it. Maybe that's why I kept doing what I was doing. Maybe I wanted to get in trouble so at least I would get noticed. Negative attention is better than no attention at all.

I remember a photograph of me as a young boy, still in diapers. I am standing in our living room in our house in Detroit. Behind me is a blond end table which was next to the couch. The top surface of the table is covered with large bath towels, which are secured to the table with what appears to be packing tape. Towels served the purpose of protecting the table from me and my little wooden hammer. I used to enjoy pounding on the top of the table with my hammer. I'm sure that I marred the surface of the table significantly before my mom came up with the idea of protecting it. She could have punished me for damaging the furniture. She could have taken away my hammer. She could have made me pay for resurfacing the table, if I had any money of my own at that early age. Or she could have withheld my future allowance until the cost of resurfacing the table was met. I don't know if she tried any disciplinary approaches. All I know is that the table, and its matching twin, survived my childhood and made it to my adult years because the towels saved it from further harm.

That little wooden hammer became famous for another infamous incident from my undisciplined early years. One morning, I took my hammer outside. For some reason unknown to me, I took my little wooden hammer and smashed the window of my mother's car. According to my mother's account of the story, I then came into the house and announced to her with great pride that I broke the car window and that I did it with my left hand. I must have been so proud of myself to be able to use my nondominant left hand. I can almost imagine the feeling of joy and accomplishment that I must have had. Sounds like another opportunity to have my hammer taken away and to be punished for doing such a terrible thing. But I got away with it. As the story would be told in my later years, it was always a source of humor, as if I had done something cute. I think I developed a reputation as being a troublemaker, and this was just typical for Csabi.

Breaking the car window was not the only thing I was known for when it came to cars. During my childhood years, cigarette and cigar smoking was popular. Television advertisements portrayed smoking as a socially accepted, even glamorous activity. Well-dressed men would light a cigarette for their stylish lady. The attractive "Cigars, cigarettes, Tiparillos" woman would stroll through the crowd at the cocktail party asking if anyone needed a smoke. "The modern smoke found in all the right places with all the right people." Edie Adams would sing her sultry song about Muriel Cigars. Cigarettes would be left out on tables for people to smoke at parties. Smoking was permitted practically everywhere. Even airplanes had smoking sections. Cars were equipped with a push-in cigarette lighter and an ash tray in the front seat. Some cars even had them in the back seat. My family had one of those cars. I used to enjoy climbing into the back seat when the car was parked at our house, pushing in the cigarette lighter, and patiently waiting for the coils to get hot. When the lighter popped out and the coils were nice and red hot, I would push the hot lighter against the vinyl material on the back of the front seat. The result of this would be a pattern of concentric circles burned into the material. It was as if I was branding steers on a cattle ranch. The mark of Csabi—forever burned into my mother's car. I can still remember the smell of the lighter as it got hot and the aroma of melting vinyl as I made my mark. I would do this quite often until the seat was covered with burned circles. I think back and wonder if anyone ever considered locking the car door, taking the lighter out of the car, or locking the lighter in the glove box. Perhaps those actions would have frustrated me so much that I would have taken my little wooden hammer and smashed the car window. Just another cute story about Csabi.

Some cars with automatic transmissions came equipped with push-button gear-shift mechanisms. Instead of having a handle on the steering column with the typical PRNDL selections, or the sportier floor shift, many automobiles had push buttons on the dashboard. This was much more compact and even futuristic looking. But I don't think the designers took into account the fascination that I would have with the buttons. I was into gadgets like many little boys, and I had a high level of curiosity as well. It wasn't enough for me to play with the buttons and push them in one at a time. No, not for Csabi. I would have to push in two or three at a time to see what would happen. Of course, what would happen would not be a good thing and my dad the auto mechanic would often have to come to the rescue.

I also had a fascination with the slot for the ignition key. If a key could fit it the slot, I was sure that other things would as well. For example, a bobby pin. Sure enough, a bobby pin would fit in quite nicely. Not only that, it could also be difficult to remove. Or it might even cause some damage to the electrical system. Just another thing for Dad the auto mechanic to have to deal with. I wonder why people didn't lock their cars with me around. I wonder why I was allowed to do the things I did and not get punished or disciplined. Perhaps I was such a monster that I frustrated the hell out of my mom and dad. I don't really know. It was just Csabi doing what Csabi does.

Another one of my all-time favorite things to do was to spit milk into the floor furnace. During the cold winter months in Detroit, the floor furnace was a nice, warm place for me to sit near. I discovered that spitting cold milk into the furnace would cause a sizzling sound. The smell of the milk was certainly less than pleasing.

Among my brother's friends, I was known as a terror as well. His friends were afraid to come into our house because I enjoyed biting them. I once socked a girl in the stomach for no apparent reason other than it was a Csabi thing. Later in life, I often felt like I grew up in my brother's shadow and that I would never be able to achieve what he did. Perhaps I was looking for a way to make my mark. Perhaps I was seeking the attention that I needed. Perhaps I felt unloved. I will never know what motivated me to do these Csabi things.

Chapter Three
My Parents

My father and mother were Hungarian Jews. Both were born in Eastern Hungary, not far from the border with Romania. My dad, Imre Goldstein, was born on January 17, 1913, in Haláp. My mom, Klára Ehrenfeld, was born on September 2, 1920, in Sáránd. The two small towns were separated by only about thirty kilometers, but my parents did not meet each other until after World War II. Both came from large families and grew up in small, rural towns. My dad grew up on a farm, and my mom's family had a small store. In 1932, typhoid fever took the lives of my mom's mother and a younger sister. My mom was also stricken with the illness, but survived. The Nazi Party began to assert its evil power throughout Europe, and life became extremely difficult for the Jews. My father joined the Hungarian Army. My mother wanted to go to school to be a dental hygienist, but that was not allowed. She became a seamstress instead. The Nazis invaded Hungary in 1944. Mom and Dad spoke very little of their experiences during the Holocaust and, whenever I wanted to learn more about what they endured, they refused to talk about it. It was not something they wanted to have to relive. Many relatives were murdered during the war. My father had only one surviving sister. My mother's family was more fortunate, and I got to know three of her sisters and a brother.

I can't even begin to imagine the lives that my parents had to lead. The effects on them must have been terrible, and I believe that they suffered from post-traumatic stress disorder, although it was never diagnosed.

My mother's father and all of her sisters were prisoners in Auschwitz. Her father was murdered by the Nazis, but all of her sisters survived. My mother always told me that she was with her sister in a forced labor camp, but this was not true. I learned only after she died that she had been keeping her experiences a secret. In fact, she and several women were on a forced march when a Hungarian guard warned them that they were to be killed and recommended that they look for ways to escape. The guard offered to take my mother to safety, and she accepted. He pretended that Mom was his sister, and she lived with his family where she worked to help take care of the family. Although she was spared from the Nazis, Mom was raped by the Hungarian guard and impregnated with his child. She had an abortion and lived with this secret for the rest of her life. She suffered with the memories of being assaulted as well as the guilt of not having to experience the Nazi horrors as the rest of her family did.

My dad led a life devoted to his work. As an

auto mechanic, he worked hard every day. On most days, he worked from 7:00 a.m. until 9:00 p.m. He came home dirty, greasy, smelling of oil and gasoline. He would have his dinner, watch TV, and fall asleep. My memories of my dad do not include many conversations. I can't recall talking about my schooling, my interest in music, and I know that we never talked about the birds and the bees. We had fun on Sundays, looking at the classified ads (in Hungarian, apróhirdetés) to find used cars to buy. He enjoyed that, and I liked getting hold of the newspaper first and scouting out the good deals. I wouldn't say that Dad was an absent father. But he didn't have much of an education, so he couldn't help me with schoolwork. He didn't have conversations with me about things I was interested in, such as baseball or music. I don't remember him coming to many of my games or concerts, since he was usually working. Although this was probably not true, I got the impression that he didn't care. What made matters worse was I always thought that he was so proud of my brother for being the first to get a high school diploma, go to college, graduate, and get a job. It seemed to me that everyone knew about him and his accomplishments. By the time I came along, I just followed in his footsteps. Even after I got my MBA and started my first job, my dad didn't ask me what I was doing or how I liked my job. He simply wanted to know if I was busy. He valued hard work, so being busy was important.

One night when I was home from college for winter break, I went to see *The Exorcist* with some friends, all of whom happened to be female. It was a midnight show, and we were all scared out of our wits by the end of the movie. I ended up driving everyone home and, when I got to the last girl's house (this girl had been my girlfriend and prom date in high school), she wanted me to walk her in because she was scared. We went in and found that her mother was awake, so we sat and talked until the sun came up. I drove home and, as I walked into my house, my dad was just leaving to go to work. Rather than being angry about me being out all night or even asking me what was going on, he said hello and said he was going to work. He didn't seem to care at all about me being gone all night. Maybe it was because I was already a college student or maybe he trusted me. But that typifies his involvement as a parent. Even when it came to learning about sex, it was Mom, not Dad, as you will read in a later chapter.

My parents led very private lives. They did not have many close friends, and they rarely socialized. My mother used to refer to herself as a greenhorn, and she must have thought that native Americans saw her as inferior. She had difficulty having close friends, and she often thought that they were using her in some way, either for her expertise at sewing or knitting. Many people adored my mother, but I got the impression that she was unable to return the feeling. I learned just recently that Mom was not a happy child even before her wartime experience. She was a sad child and was given the nickname fa kutya (wooden dog) by her father because she was emotionless and reminded him of the statue of a dog.

Because of her Holocaust experience, my mother had an intense hatred for Germans. We never owned a product made in Germany and she wouldn't allow a German car to be parked in our driveway. Mom wanted no part of an automobile that was to be the car of the German people. There was a family with a German name who lived directly across the street from us. We didn't know them well but the father also worked at a service station and I used to play baseball with his boys. I thought the boys were different because they weren't Jewish. Since my school was predominantly Jewish and they lived in a different school district, I didn't see them very often. I used to see the mother of the family washing the bricks of their house, cleaning the patio furniture, and washing their cars. My mother would comment that they were typically German because of their cleanliness and everything had to look just so. I grew up thinking that Germans were different in a bad way not just because of the Holocaust. Even at the age of thirty-three, when I visited Hungary, I hated the sight of one particular German car, with East German plates, parked in our hotel parking lot. If I ever saw the man who drove it, I would turn away and not say a word of greeting to him. I pictured him in an SS uniform and it seemed to fit him well.

My parents had issues with money and status. We never had a lot of money but I never wanted for anything. My parents were able to support me through college and I know they saved their money carefully. Seven years after my parents came to America, there was a revolution in Hungary in 1956. Many Hungarians made their way to America at that time. My parents sponsored a family to come to America, and they settled in Detroit. They found work in the meat-packing business in Detroit's Eastern Market. They had a successful business and I remember them driving luxury cars. My mother appeared envious of them since they came to America later and seemed to have more money than they knew what to do with.

Because of their Holocaust experience, my parents had doubts about religion, their faith and belief, and the existence of God. Although my brother went to Yeshiva and I attended a religious school, we did not belong to a synagogue and we rarely attended services. I was an excellent student in religious school but my teachers always stressed the importance of synagogue attendance. I still have vivid memories of my first time being dropped off at a synagogue by my mom (she would not come in). I was wearing a nice sweater and a pair of slacks while all of the other boys from my class were wearing a coat and tie. I immediately felt different and not as good as the rest of the boys. Of course, no one said anything at all to me about my attire. I just reached the conclusion that my mom should have known better and should have bought me a suit. I was angry with her when she picked me up and we went to buy a suit so I would feel better about myself.

When it became time to plan my Bar Mitzvah, a good friend of ours arranged to have it take place in her synagogue. I prepared diligently and was ready on May 13, 1967, to become a man in the eyes of Judaism. I was called up for my Aliyah and I chanted the blessing before the Torah reading. I knew my Torah reading perfectly and was preparing to chant it when a voice came from behind me. A man standing behind me was chanting my Torah portion. I was stunned, and I glanced down at my mother sitting in the front row. She had a look of surprise on her face as well. I proceeded to recite the blessing after the Torah reading and chanted a flawless haftarah. After the service, my mother spoke with the president of the congregation about why I was not allowed to read from the Torah. He stated that only synagogue members were given that privilege. In other words, if you pay your dues, you get the full package. Being nonmembers, we just didn't measure up to their standards. We weren't good enough for them. The memory of that day in 1967 has stayed with me as a slap in the face and a blow to my self-esteem.

Robert Gray

The occasion of my Bar Mitzvah marked my passage into manhood from a Jewish perspective. It also marked the end of my Jewish education and the questioning of my faith for many years. After my Bar Mitzvah, my mother explained that she and Dad wanted me to know that I was Jewish, to understand what it meant to be Jewish, and know about my Jewish heritage. She also told me that she and Dad didn't believe in anything after their Holocaust experiences. There would no longer be Sabbath dinners and candles on Friday evening. We would no longer celebrate the holidays. I didn't have to go to synagogue anymore. She left it up to me to choose my Judaic path. While many of my close friends belonged to Jewish youth groups and continued to grow as Jews, I chose not to. My Bar Mitzvah was the end of my Jewish journey and I didn't understand what I was missing until much later in life. It would be about twenty-six years later when I finally read from the Torah. I retaught myself the trop (the musical symbols) and started reading on Mondays and Thursdays at morning minyan. I eventually read Torah on Rosh Hashanah and several Shabbatot, and have become a more active member of the synagogue than I ever dreamed I would. I have led Rosh Hashanah services, began attending Torah study classes, and became a synagogue board officer. Although my parents gave up on faith and religion, I think they would be proud of me.

Chapter 4
Shyness and Fears

Although I was rambunctious and a trouble-maker, I was also very shy and fearful. Academically, my elementary school years were quite successful. I excelled in every subject (with the exception of cursive writing) and was always considered to be one of the smartest kids in the class. Athletically, I was pretty good at baseball and was the captain of the best fifth-grade baseball team at my school. I also had the advantage of being a left-handed batter, so I usually got to hit the ball to the worst fielder on the other team, who was stuck in right field. I enjoyed playing little league baseball since I was a good hitter and pretty good in the field too. But my extreme shyness caused me problems when it came to fundraising for our program. In order to afford the uniforms and equipment, each player had to sell Optimist Club pens that were shaped like baseball bats. Each year, I would be given my allotment of ten pens to sell. I used to walk around the neighborhood trying to muster up the courage to actually knock on someone's door and ask them if they would buy a pen. Sometimes I would just throw the pens away and ask my mom if she would give me money for something. Or I would get my mom to buy the pens so I wouldn't have to try to sell them. I never told anyone that I was afraid to approach neighbors and ask them to buy a pen.

I always wanted to be like my older brother. He was seven years older and was my idol. When he would walk to school, I would walk to the end of the street, carrying my books so that I could be like him. He and I used to sleep in the same bedroom, and I would often have trouble going to sleep until he came home safely. The fact that there was a pattern in the wood of our bedroom closet door that looked like a great big mean dog may have had something to do with it as well. Both of us used to like to keep that closet open at bedtime. Sometimes, if I couldn't sleep, I would climb into bed with my dad. He and Mom never slept in the same room for as long as I can remember. But I would never stay long because of his loud snoring and the ever-present smell of oil and gasoline that he brought home with him from work. I understood why Mom slept in her own room.

All in all, childhood wasn't bad. At least it didn't appear to be bad. I was intelligent and excelled in all subjects in school. I began playing the clarinet in the fifth grade and I was always one of the best clarinet players in the band. My teachers liked me because I didn't get into trouble in school. I was pretty good at baseball, and I hit many home runs. I was also a pitcher with a pretty nasty slow curveball. I could throw pretty hard, but I was afraid I would hit someone in the head, so I dialed my fastball down quite a bit. I still remember a game that we won 1-0 against one of the best teams in the league. My friends on the opposing team couldn't hit me because they were used to faster pitching in batting practice.

I had a keen sense of humor and the kids in school thought I was funny. But inside my brain, the story had a different feeling. I was afraid of making a mistake or being wrong. I was fat and many of the kids picked on me or teased me because of it. None of the cool kids were fat, so I knew I could never be a cool kid.

My shyness made me afraid to ask questions or ask for help. I recall a time when my mom transferred me to a different Hebrew school. At the first school, I was taught the Ashkenazic form of Hebrew. At my new school, they used the Sephardic form, so I had to learn a different way of reading and pronouncing certain consonants and vowels. One of the assignments was to translate some of the passages from the Torah into English. I had no idea that I could simply look up the passage in my *Chumash* and find the translation. So, I took out my handy pocket Hebrew dictionary to look up the words. I still remember the passage from Genesis chapter 12, "Go forth from your land and from your birthplace and from your father's house, to the land that I will show you." What I didn't know then was that the Hebrew language uses prefixes and suffixes which are added to the root word to make a new word. For example, "from your land" appears as one word in Hebrew but it is actually the root word "eretz," the prefix meaning "from," and the suffix meaning "your." So, my handy little pocket dictionary didn't have the word I was looking for. As a matter of fact, it had very few of the words I was looking for. I was frantic. I was crying to my mother asking her what kind of school she was sending me to. I was the smartest student at my previous school, and now I was going to look like an idiot. I went to class feeling so scared that the teacher would call on me and I wouldn't know the answer. He didn't, thank God, but I found out that all of the other kids knew the answers. Then I found out that the answers were all in the *Chumash*. I never worried about that again. At least not about that.

The whole "cool kid" thing was a problem for me. I idolized the cool kids. To be a cool kid, you had to have a bigger house than mine, you had to have more money than my family did, you had to dress better than I did, you had to be better looking than I was, you had to be more confident than I was, you had to be more mature than I was, and you had to be popular with the opposite sex. I don't know what measuring scale I used to make these comparisons but, in my head, I made them. Certain kids were just cool and, to me, they were unapproachable, untouchable, and out of my league. Most of these cool kids came from what I called the other side of town, or the Manor. Although the distance from my house to the other side of town was an easy bike ride, to me it was like entering another world. The homes were bigger, the cars were nicer, the landscape was better. They had better jobs and more money. Same zip code but different neighborhood. I used to ride my bike along the streets in the cool neighborhoods just so I might get a glimpse of a cool kid. I might even wave at them and get a wave in return. What a feeling! One day, I actually rode by and there were several cool kids outside. I stopped to say hello (what nerve, right?). To my surprise, I was asked to come inside. Cool kids, boys and girls, asking me to come inside. One of the boys was older than I was, so I was in awe of him. He was already in junior high school and he was a jock. All I can remember about that day was sitting on a couch with the cool kids and watching TV. Some innocent tickling was going on, and I was in heaven.

I actually did have some close friends when I was a kid. I played T-ball and little league baseball, and I used to go to the school during the summer for recreation. But I would rarely be the one to initiate things. If a friend came over, we would go outside and play and I enjoyed myself. It was unusual for me to take the first step and go to one of their houses. I became an expert at playing games all by myself to pass the time when I was alone. It didn't matter if it was a two-player game or not. I played both sides. Even if the game was something like baseball, where opposing mana-gers had to make decisions for their teams. I would make the decisions for both sides as if I didn't know what the other manager was going to do. I loved to set up plays with my tabletop NHL hockey set and practice them over and over again. It's tough to play a two-player action game alone, but I made it work. I was also a nut for statistics. When I played solitaire, I would keep track of how many cards were placed on each ace to see if the first one placed usually got the most cards. With my marble raceway game, I would put the four marbles in the same order time after time to record their finishing positions to see if the first marble in the front of the starting line had the advantage. I would sort my baseball cards in every order possible based on the statistics on the back just for the fun of it. I used to throw rubber balls against the brick of my house in the backyard to practice my pitching. I only broke the basement window a few times when my pitches were low and away. I played the same game in our living room, using a pillow as my target. I developed a one-person hockey game in the basement using a golf club and a golf ball. I would hit the ball against the wall and would have to stop it from getting to the stairs behind me. The basement floor tiles got marked up, the cinder-block wall would chip away from the impact of the golf ball, and I got hit in the head a few times. But it was a fun game.

When I did play with a friend, I was usually better than they were at the things that we did. That was important to me since I was such a poor sport when it came to losing. I remember playing a card game called Casino with my dad and he had this way of teasing me when he was winning, which was quite often. He always seemed to have the right card at the right time. I can still hear him saying, "Thirteen, thirteen, tableau." I would get upset, cry, throw the cards, and refuse to play. But it gave me great pleasure when I was able to throw harder than my older brother and beat him at ping-pong or table hockey. I didn't know how to have a good time unless I was winning.

My brother was a very intelligent young fellow. In high school, he excelled in math and went on to major in mathematics in college. I wanted to be like him, so being intelligent was important to me. He used to have friends over to our house to study. I used to like to hang around them as much as they would tolerate. Some of his friends called me "Child Prodigy," so I guess I impressed them with what I knew. My brother had a different description of me, which was probably more accurate. He would describe me as blasé. Perhaps he saw something that others didn't. I was rarely angry, usually low-key and nonchalant. The accurate description was most likely dysthymic. According to the Mayo Clinic, "Dysthymia is a mild but long-term (chronic) form of depression. Symptoms usually last for at least two years, and often for much longer than that. Dysthymia interferes with your ability to function and enjoy life. With dysthymia, you may lose interest in normal daily activities, feel hopeless, lack productivity, and have low self-esteem and an overall feeling of inadequacy. People with dysthymia are often thought of as being overly critical, constantly complaining, and incapable of having fun." That sounds a lot like me, except for the part about constantly complaining. I kept things inside. I was too afraid to complain. I was too embarrassed to admit that I needed help or to ask for it. I chose to suffer in silence.

When my brother was a freshman at Michigan, he invited me up for a little brother weekend. I was excited to spend a weekend on campus and to attend a football game. When we went to the game, I had a ticket that said "Student" on it. I was so afraid that they would not let me in because I was a fifth grader, obviously not a university student. When we got to the ticket taker at the turnstile, I handed him the ticket. He took it with no questions asked. I sighed with relief and said, "I can't believe he took my ticket." I was so insecure and thought I would get into trouble for using an improper ticket. I hated the thought of being in trouble.

My brother had a very expensive stereo system. It had a turntable with a weight hanging from a string for balance. It had a reel-to-reel tape player, an amplifier with an oscilloscope, and two massive speakers. He gave me permission to listen to his tapes as long as I was careful. I enjoyed listening to his music and watching the oscilloscope display. I can still remember listening to "Getting Better" by

The Beatles and watching the oscilloscope react to each quarter-note chord on the guitar. One time, I was rewinding a tape and I hit the play button before the tape had completely stopped. The tape didn't break but something happened to it so that, when it got to that point in the music, the tape would stop. I was terrified. I thought I had ruined the tape forever, and I obviously didn't use the stereo system carefully. I was so afraid to tell him that I ruined his tape, so I said nothing, as if the tape might heal itself on its own and all would be well. Hopefully, he would never listen to that tape again and I would be spared. Then, one fateful evening, he decided to listen to that tape. I was shaking with fear, waiting for the dreadful moment when the tape would stop. When it did stop, he went to check out what had happened. He noticed that something was wrong with the tape which was causing it to stop. It appeared that the tape had been damaged or stretched in some way. I couldn't keep it in any longer. I sheepishly said that I knew what had happened to the tape. I told him what I had done and started crying and apologizing. As it turned out, it was easily repairable and it would play just fine. I didn't realize then that he could have just rerecorded the album if he had to. All I knew was that I had done something wrong and didn't want to admit to it. I was afraid I would be punished and that my brother would hate me. That thought pattern of not being liked if I did something wrong would repeat itself many times over the years to come.

Chapter Five
Elementary School

In Detroit, the schools were kindergarten through eighth grade. I began my school career at a K–12 school in Detroit as a kindergarten student. One day in kindergarten, some of the kids were teasing each other and saying that their moms were not going to come and pick them up to go home. This really affected me and I remember crying hysterically thinking that I would be locked in the school all night long and that my mom didn't care about me. Of all of my 180 or so days in kindergarten, that is the only thing I can remember. I don't remember the teacher's name, the appearance of the room, or any of the kids. But that one terrifying memory lingers.

We moved to Oak Park in April 1960. I had started first grade in Detroit in January, so, for me to be with kids my age, I had to wait until September to start first grade in Oak Park. We were part of the "White Flight" out of Detroit, and Oak Park was a quaint little, mostly Jewish community just to the north. We lived near Nine Mile Road, not far from the road made famous several years ago by Eminem. By this time, at the tender young age of six, I had already developed some sort of a concern about germs. I didn't like the idea of taking a bath in the tub of our new house since the tub used to belong to someone else and they used it. My mom assured me that she had cleaned it and, although it looked shiny and spotless, it took some time for me to want to take a bath. This phobia, if that is what it is, has stayed with me all my life. I still won't take a bath in a hotel tub and strange toilets cause me to fret when I travel. My fear of germs will appear several more times in my life story.

Something happened to me when I began going to school. I never really thought much about it until I began writing this book, and I have never tried to make sense of it. The rambunctious, attention-seeking, troublemaking Csabi vanished. He was replaced by a shy, quiet, nervous, afraid-to-cause-trouble little boy named Robert. During elementary school, I was intelligent but stayed in the background. I was often thought of as a teacher's pet and didn't get into trouble. I was actually afraid to get in trouble. I didn't what to feel ashamed for doing something wrong. I didn't want to feel embarrassment for not knowing the correct answers or not being prepared for the assignment. I did my homework religiously, practiced my clarinet daily, without prodding from my parents. I wanted to be the best and the smartest. I followed the rules. I was a model student. I don't know why this happened. Perhaps, at home, I was getting away with bloody murder so I kept acting out to test the limits. Having no consequences for my actions, perhaps I felt that it was okay to be a terror. Perhaps I felt that the teachers presented themselves as authority figures and I saw that discipline was real. A trip to the principal's office could really happen. Whatever the reason, the biting, punching, destructive Csabi was gone, replaced by the meek, mild-mannered, goody-two-shoes, teacher's pet Robert.

Human memory has always fascinated me. I wish I knew why I remember the things that I do. I believe that people who deal with depression are more likely to remember negative thoughts or events. Or, at least, we have a filter that colors the way we remember events. When I think about elementary school, I mainly remember wanting to fit in. I hated being teased about things that made me different from other kids. Yes, I wanted to be smart. I wanted to be the best. I just didn't want to be different.

My first-grade teacher was Mrs. Adams. I don't have many clear memories of my first-grade year. This was my first year at my elementary school. I didn't know any of the kids, but I do remember one of the first interactions I had with one of them. Our desks were arranged in rectangles so that we directly faced another student. The first student who said something to me was a young boy named Joey. The first thing he said to me was a taunt, a tease, a put-down. He noticed something about my attire and he spoke to me. "Ha ha, you have to wear suspenders!" I didn't know that suspenders were considered weird, or that belts were the thing that all normal Oak Park first graders wore. All I knew was that Joey made me feel different, less than, and embarrassed. And so it begins, my story of feeling less than others, not good enough, and being different.

I never wanted to be different, even if being different was a good thing. In the snowy and icy winter months, I wore boots to school, as did most, if not all, of the kids. Before going out for recess or going home, it was quite an ordeal to get all of the kids dressed to go outside. We would all sit on the floor by the coat hooks and put on our boots, gloves, hats, and coats. It was crowded, and we didn't have a lot of room to move around. The most difficult thing was to get those black rubber boots to slip onto our shoes. The teacher often had to help with this struggle. Of course, if I was having difficulty, I would feel embarrassed that I needed help. My mother had a solution to the boot problem. She would have me put plastic bags over my shoes, and then it was easy to slide my feet into my boots. It worked very well and made things easier for me. But the other kids didn't have plastic bags on their shoes, so I felt weird about it. I didn't want them to see that I was different, even though the plastic bags were a great idea. Being different was not a good thing. I could get teased or singled out.

My second-grade teacher was Miss Bailey.

Second grade was the first time that someone felt that I needed help. I remember Miss Bailey as being a young, blond woman. One day, my teacher gave me a sealed envelope to take home to my mom. She said that she was sending a recipe home with me for my mom. I delivered it to Mom as I was instructed. It was not a recipe. It was a note to my mom telling her that I was extremely shy and was having trouble socially in class. I don't know exactly what the note said, nor do I know when my mom told me about it. But I do remember what my mom said to me about the note. She told me that this young teacher didn't know what she was talking about and that there was nothing wrong with me. She said that I didn't need any help, and that was the end of that. I don't know if my father knew anything about it but, if he did, we never spoke about it. So, help was not forthcoming. It's possible that my mom truly didn't think I needed help. Or, perhaps she felt like we couldn't afford it. Or, perhaps she was in denial that any of us needed anything. I don't recall what I was feeling back then, but I learned that if something was bothering me, I should keep it to myself. I'm sure had I started to see a counselor or therapist back then, I would have been ashamed and embarrassed for being different. My mom used to like to use the expression "suffer in silence." I got good at that.

Even as a young boy in elementary school, I was extremely competitive and needed to be the best and the smartest in my class. There was a girl named Julie in my second-grade class who was my big rival. She was very smart, and I competed with her to be in the best reading group, math group, and to beat her in spelling bees. One day, Julie was no longer in my class and I was astonished to find out that she had been promoted to the next grade. I was furious about it (internally, of course) since I felt like I should have also been promoted. I was as smart as she was. Why was I not promoted? I decided that the reason was that her handwriting was much better than mine. I didn't see much of Julie after that, and she eventually moved to another school district. As an adult, I still remembered how she was promoted ahead of me and, out of curiosity, I searched for her on the internet to see if I could find out where she was. When I found her, I discovered that she was born in 1953, the year before me. She was older than everyone else in my grade, so she was probably promoted to be with her age group. For about fifty years, I felt I had been slighted and held a grudge against Julie based on incorrect and childish assumptions. I assumed that I was not good enough.

As I think back on my childhood years, I see a puzzling paradox. In some ways, I didn't want to be special, different, or noticed. I wanted to be like the other kids, no suspenders, no bags on the shoes, nothing weird to be teased about. Yet, in other ways, I wanted to be special, different, or noticed. I wanted to stand out academically, I wanted to be noticed for my abilities, I wanted to be the best. Perhaps not such a puzzling paradox after all. My self-worth was based on the thoughts and feelings of others rather than a belief in myself. I needed to be recognized by kids and teachers as the best. Being teased for being smart was an ego boost for me. Being better than the rest was where I wanted to be. Where I had to be. Getting 100 percent on my homework, quizzes, and assignments was the only acceptable score. Perfection. Not for my mom or dad, not for my teachers, but for me.

My third-grade teacher was Mrs. Cramer, and I had most of the same classmates from the previous year. I was happy that I was with mostly the same kids and didn't have to try to make new friends. I liked Mrs. Cramer, and I was one of the smartest kids in the class. I had a pretty good singing voice, so I was a tenor in the choir. I started to learn how to read music, and I enjoyed rehearsing and singing for the school in concerts. My love for music is one of the things I am most grateful for in my life.

My fourth-grade teacher was Miss Durocher. I remember her as an overweight woman who perspired a lot under her arms. In November of my fourth-grade year, President John F. Kennedy was assassinated. I remember it like it was yesterday. There was commotion in the hallway, and Miss Durocher went out to see what was happening.

When she came back in, she was crying and told us that the president had been shot. I liked President Kennedy, and I was stunned at the news. I remember writing a note about his assassination to take home to my mother, thinking that she would not have heard the news. We were dismissed from school early that day, which was a Friday. For the rest of the weekend, the world was focused on the assassination and all three of our television stations covered it around the clock. Fourth grade was a good year for me academically. Miss Durocher started teaching us French, which I studied through high school. I was very good at math, so she let me work ahead in the textbook and learn at my own pace. We also started learning how to play the song flute. It was much like a recorder, and it gave me my first opportunity to learn how to play an instrument. I demonstrated a strong ability for playing the song flute and for figuring out how to play songs by ear. I had fun figuring out harmonies and playing some of the top forty songs of the day. And, of course, I felt good about being good at it.

My fifth-grade teacher, Mrs. Easterly, was quite different from my previous teachers. She had a raspy voice and a temper. I think I was afraid of her at the beginning, which increased my desire to stay out of trouble. She turned out to be okay, but I had to get used to her. In fifth grade, I started learning how to play the clarinet in the school band. When I got my clarinet, which my mom rented from the music store, I remember being intrigued by all of the shiny silver keys. The instrument sat in the case in five separate pieces, and I had no idea how to assemble it. I figured I would learn how to do it in band class. As it turned out, assembling it almost caused me to quit before ever getting started. The band director, Mr. Reed, started showing us how to assemble our instruments. I was having so many problems that I began to cry and was ready to give up. I felt so embarrassed that I couldn't put my horn together and other kids could. I felt envious of the brass players and saxophonists who only had to put a mouthpiece on and they were ready to go. The pieces of my horn just wouldn't cooperate. Mr. Reed came to help me and showed me how to apply cork grease to the joints of my clarinet. Like magic, everything worked like a charm, and I was ready to go. Of course, rather than raising my hand and asking for help, I had to be stubborn and do it myself and get upset when I couldn't do it.

Fifth grade was also the year that all of the students spent a week out of the school year at camp. I had never been to a sleep-away camp and was not a fan of the outdoors, so I was not looking forward to this experience. I was especially concerned about using the bathroom. I can't imagine that too many of the kids in my class were thinking a lot about the toilet when the busses took us to the camp, but I was. I don't remember anything about my stay at camp except for "bug" juice and the bathroom. The bathroom in our bunk was a screened-in area that provided a bit of privacy, but there were flies and mosquitoes flying around. As far as I was concerned, it was not good enough for me to use it. So, I pretty much made up my mind that I was not going to have a bowel movement from Monday morning through Friday afternoon. I was just going to have to hold it in. I managed to make it through Wednesday night, but I didn't feel well on Thursday morning. I was taken to see the nurse and after a quick exam, she asked me if I wanted to go home. I told her nothing about my bathroom situation and said that I wanted to go home. My mom came and picked me up and took me home. When we got home, I had one of the best bowel movements of my young life and I felt fine. I stayed home Friday since the kids were still at camp. I can still remember looking out my bedroom window and seeing the school busses arriving to bring them home from camp.

Fifth grade was also the year when I took a real liking to girls. I started having crushes on some of the girls in my class. Up until that time, I had friends who were girls and I would sometimes go to their houses to play. But now, I felt an attraction to the opposite sex. We had a new girl in our class. She was a pretty girl with long hair, and I thought she was very cute. I wanted to impress her with the French I had learned in the fourth grade, and I told her that her name was actually a French word. I was so proud of myself. Little did I know, but her father was an archaeologist and she had spent summers in Italy and France and was fluent in both languages. I don't remember what she said about my comment about her name, but she and I were good friends all through high school. She played the flute, so we saw each other every day in band. Although I always liked her a lot, I never asked her out on a date. She would be one of many who fell into that category. I guess I was afraid of rejection.

In fifth grade, I began to show some aptitude for baseball. I had played T-ball and little league baseball in the summer and was pretty good. I was overweight and couldn't run fast, but I could hit and pitch. Being a left-handed hitter was an advantage since right field, where I usually hit the ball, was the place where the least talented kids typically played. So, I hit a lot of home runs to right field. In gym class, all of the fifth-grade classes had a draft to select players for their baseball teams. I was a captain of one of our teams, and a girl named Jennifer was captain of the other team. Jennifer got to pick first, and she selected a friend of hers. I don't remember if the friend was a girl or a boy, but she gave me the chance to pick the other really good left-handed hitter in my class, Ricky. With Ricky and I on the same team, we couldn't lose. Sure enough, our team went on to beat all of the other fifth-grade class teams. It meant a lot to me to be on the best team and to fit in for something athletic.

Sixth grade was probably one of the best years of my young life. My teacher was Mrs. Farley. I think she was new to the school since I had never heard of her. I rode past her classroom on my bicycle a few days before school started and I thought she looked like a witch. She had long, streaked hair and a pointy nose. I thought she would be a terrible teacher, but she turned out to be my favorite. The only problem I had with Mrs. Farley was that she had a condition that required her to eat during the day. She had a rule that if she could eat in class, then so could we. I gained a lot of weight that year, trading sandwiches for candy. Sixth grade was a fun year for me. I was one of the oldest kids in the school since we were going to junior high school for seventh grade. I was still one of the smartest in the class, and I was one of the best clarinet players in the band. I was still painfully shy, and I could feel the distinction between the cool kids and the group I was in. I was very interested in girls but so afraid to say anything. My class often had dance parties at the end of the week, and I was one of the kids who played the records and watched. At one of the dance parties, we played a slow song by The Mamas and the Papas called "Monday, Monday." Somehow I ended up dancing with Stacy, the girl I thought was the coolest girl ever. I think I got pushed into dancing with her. I'm sure I wouldn't have had the nerve to ask her myself. Slow dancing with Stacy was like being in heaven for me. I never danced with her again, but I'll never forget the one and only dance with her.

Sixth grade was the year for sex education. I never talked about sex with my parents at this point and was quite naïve about the whole subject. All of the boys went into Mr. Ripley's room to learn all about sex. I can't remember how it was presented to us, but I remember that I didn't get it. I understood something about a sperm and an egg getting together, but the process was unclear to me. I remember thinking that a girl could get pregnant if I touched her arm, and somehow one of my sperm could find its way to one of her eggs. I didn't know how that could happen or where I kept these little sperm, but I joked about it with some of the girls. I knew nothing about lovemaking or reproduction at all. Whatever Mr. Ripley said to us, I obviously didn't get it. When I got home in the afternoon, my mom asked me if I had any questions. I told her that I didn't understand what I had heard. She started to explain it to me, and then things started to click. All of a sudden, I realized that she was talking about fucking. I started to understand that having sex and fucking were the same thing. I thought this was sinful, terrible, and I didn't understand that married people who love each other do this. I was so confused and angry at my mother for having sex. How could she and my dad do such a thing? When she was finished explaining it to me and making sure that the shock had worn off, I said something that would never be forgotten. "Well, I guess it's not so bad. You only did it twice." Once

Robert Gray

for my brother and once for me. I still thought it was sinful and dirty, but I was willing to forgive my mom since she only did it twice. That was the only conversation I ever had with my mom about sex. My dad and I never spoke of it at all. There were many conversations I never had with my dad, a fact which I will always regret.

Chapter Six
Junior High School

September of 1966 marked a major transition in my young life. I was leaving the comfortable surroundings of elementary school, where I knew most of the students and teachers, for the horrors of junior high school. No longer would I be one of the oldest students in the school, one of the sixth graders who ruled the roost. I was heading for seventh grade in a school that, although it was right next door to my elementary school, represented a whole new world for me. No longer would I be able to stay in one room all day. Now I had to navigate my way around this strange place for homeroom and seven class periods. I had to remember my locker combination and figure out how to be on time to all my classes. When would I be able to stop at my locker? Would I have to carry my books to all of my classes to avoid the shame of being late to class? Which route should I take to make sure I would be on time? What if I got lost? What if I couldn't remember the room number or where the class was? This new and mysterious school building was rectangular and only had two floors, so navigation was not really an issue, but I worried about it nonetheless. And now, being a lowly seventh grader amongst a bunch of eighth and ninth graders was scary too. I had to start out at the bottom of the ladder again. Some of these kids were fourteen or fifteen years old, and I was a dorky twelve-year-old kid. We were also required to take physical education in junior high school. That meant we had to change to gym clothes and take showers in front of each other. I think this scared me more than anything. There was also the issue of meeting so many new kids. Several elementary schools fed into my junior high school, so I would have to meet and compete with many new kids. I knew some of them through my involvement in the summer band programs or baseball, but there were so many others who were complete strangers to me.

By far, the biggest change between elementary school and junior high school was the integration of black and white kids. The 1960s was a decade known for tension, unrest, and rebellion. President Kennedy was assassinated in 1963. The Vietnam War raged on amidst protests and demonstrations. We were about to embark on the Age of Aquarius, and the use of drugs was common. The 1960s also saw some of the most violent race riots in our history. Martin Luther King Jr. became famous for his "I Have a Dream" speech in 1963. Nonviolent protests and movements often led to encounters with law enforcement and military personnel. Many American cities experienced riots, looting, bloodshed, and death as the Civil Rights Movement was met with opposition. In 1967, during the summer before eighth grade, the city of Detroit suffered through several days of violence, fear, and destruction. But, the summer of 1966, just before seventh grade, the Kercheval "mini-riot" occurred. Although the Detroit leaders tried to portray this as just an incident, it was a sign that there was certainly something brewing. The Tactical Mobile Unit of the Detroit Police Department was called in to quell the revolution and peace was restored without a shot being fired.

The town of Oak Park, where I grew up and went to school, was a suburb of Detroit. Its southernmost border was Eight Mile Road. Anything south of Eight Mile Road was Detroit. In the 1960s, Oak Park was mostly white and mostly Jewish. When the White Flight from Detroit began, Oak Park was one of the first destinations. My parents moved there in 1960 from the northwest side of Detroit. Most of my friends and neighbors were Jewish, as were most of my teachers. There were several synagogues in the area and I attended Hebrew school, as did most of my friends. But living so close to Detroit, I was certainly aware of a different world that existed just a few miles away. I saw it whenever I went to a Detroit Tigers baseball game. Tiger Stadium was a wonderful place to watch my favorite team, but I felt unsafe when walking to our car. Located at the corner of Michigan and Trumbull, it was not in a very good neighborhood. I also saw it whenever I went to a Detroit Red Wings game. The Red Wings played in the old Olympia Stadium, located on Grand River near Grand Boulevard. I remember we would park our car on the street in the neighborhood and pay a kid to watch the car so nothing would happen to it.

Not far from Oak Park was an area called Royal Oak Township. The Township area covered about 0.55 square miles and in 1960, its population was about eight thousand, mostly black, and shrinking. I remember driving through the Township many times and noticing the rows of apartments and the general poor appearance of the area: a much different community compared to Oak Park. The Township had a school called Washington Elementary School. In 1960, Governor of Michigan G. Mennen Williams consolidated the Washington School District, along with its elementary school, into the Oak Park School District because the Washington district no longer had sufficient taxes to pay for senior high school services, and no area school districts voluntarily took its students for high school. Having no secondary school in the community, the Township kids were divided into two groups. One group would be bussed to the Ferndale School District while the other would be bussed to the Oak Park School District. In the midst of the Civil Rights Movement with rioting and violence, and enormous tension and fear, we had to find a way to understand each other and accept each other within the four walls of Walt Whitman Junior High School.

And so it began. My ascendancy to the seventh

grade at Walt Whitman Junior High School. No longer would I be able to walk home for lunch every day and watch *Jeopardy* with my mom. No more lunchtime bike rides to the pharmacy to buy baseball cards. No more recess. No more being on top of the pyramid as a sixth grader. So many changes. So much uncertainty. So many things to fear. Would I still be one of the smart kids? Would anybody like me? Would I fit in? Would I survive? Would I overcome my shyness?

On the morning of the first day of seventh grade, I woke up quite early. Although my walk to school took no more than about ten minutes and homeroom started at 8:20 a.m., I set my alarm for 6:30 a.m. I was not concerned with sleeping in or not hearing my alarm clock. I needed at least an hour to sit in the bathroom. I never liked public bathrooms, and I was sure that those at the school would not be to my liking either. I had to sit in the bathroom for an hour, whether I had to go or not, to make sure that I was empty and would not have to use the school bathroom. I later found out that there were other reasons to be afraid of the bathroom, such as getting beat up or having your money stolen from you. But on that first morning, I just had to go to school "on empty." I followed this routine pretty much all through my three years of junior high school. I remember listening to the transistor radio while sitting in the bathroom to hear news reports about the assassinations of Martin Luther King Jr. and Robert Kennedy when

I was in the eighth grade, in my second year of junior high school. I was convinced this hour in the bathroom was required for me to be able to function in school. I would rather go home sick than have to sit in the school bathroom. And I did go home sick on a couple of occasions just to be able to use my very own toilet.

The school day started with homeroom, where attendance was taken. My homeroom teacher was Mr. Orton, an art teacher, who looked like he might have been a football player. He had a big wooden paddle that he liked to use on the behinds of kids who misbehaved. I made sure never to misbehave in his homeroom. Academically, I did very well in the seventh grade. I took the most advanced math and science classes and excelled in band. I even sang in the choir and the boys' ensemble. I was selected to sing second tenor and, at first, I was upset that I was not good enough to be a first tenor. In band, being a first clarinet is better than being a second clarinet, and I thought the same held true in choir. Little did I know that I was selected as second tenor because my voice was changing and I could sing lower. Once I understood that, I felt better that I didn't have to sing the high male part.

Physical education was altogether another story. First of all, we had to wear jock straps. I found this to be embarrassing for some reason, and I remember the gym teacher would sometimes make us show him that we had them on. We each had a locker in the locker room where we had to change into our gym clothes. We had to have a combination lock to make sure that our belongings were safe. On the very first day of gym class, when I returned to my locker to change back into my clothes, I found that my lock was open and my clothes were gone. I went to the gym teacher who told me that my lock had not been locked and he had done a locker room check. He took the clothes out of any unlocked locker and returned them to the owners, along with a whack on the butt with a wiffle ball bat. So, I had to bend over and be unceremoniously smacked on the behind to get my clothes back and to be reminded never to leave my locker unlocked again. I was so ashamed to be singled out for this failure. Fortunately, the gym teacher knew me from elementary school and took it easy on me since he knew I was a good kid. Just a small whack with the plastic bat and I double and triple checked my lock every day after that. Gym class was also hard for me because I was fat and not very athletic. I absolutely hated playing "shirts and skins" basketball if I had to remove my shirt. I'm pretty sure that I had bigger boobs than many seventh-grade girls, and I was very self-conscious about it. I was teased a lot for being overweight. I was terrible at tumbling and track and field. I never looked forward to gym class unless we were playing baseball or softball. But the absolute worst thing about gym class was the showers. It was in the shower that my inadequacies were most noticeable. Some of these young men in gym class had developed much quicker than I had, and that made me feel small (pun intended). That gave the boys something else to tease me about and make me feel bad about myself.

I had become a pretty good little league ball player. Although I was overweight and slow, I could hit well and was a decent fielder. I was blessed with good coordination, which made up for my lack of speed. One early spring day, I saw an announcement for baseball team tryouts. I was interested in going to the first meeting, but I was afraid that the training would be too difficult. I couldn't run very far without having to stop and walk, and I didn't think I would make the team. On top of that, the school required a physical examination by a doctor and I didn't think my mom would want to take me for the exam. Despite my misgivings, I went to the first meeting. One of the boys saw me walk in and asked me why I was coming to the meeting. I said that I wanted to play on the team. Some of the boys chuckled, and one asked me what position I thought I would play. I already knew who the pitcher would be, and I knew I would never beat him out, so I said shortstop. One boy exclaimed that shortstop was already taken, and the laughter continued. Rather than give it the old junior high school try, I turned around and shuffled out of the room with my head hung low, never to give baseball another thought.

I did not have many black students in my classes and was not particularly friendly with very many of them. I was bullied and picked on a bit, especially in gym class, where one of the black students used to like to throw me to the ground, get on top of me, and punch my arm over and over again. I was afraid to say anything about it because I thought it would be worse if he got in trouble for it. The other students didn't get involved either. The bullying finally stopped when I showed him the bruises he had inflicted on my arm. I guess it surprised him that he was hurting me so much, so he stopped.

Junior high school life became easier after the first year. I continued to excel in class and in the band. I was taking advanced math and science and began to learn French. My social life was quite limited. I attended a few of the school dances, but I usually just walked around or talked with friends. I liked many girls, but I was too shy to even consider going out on a date. Some of the kids were "going around" with each other, but that was something I only dreamed about. I would never have the courage to ask a girl to "go around" with me.

I was not one of the cool kids and that fact was painfully made clear to me before my Bar Mitzvah. My classmates and I turned thirteen during the seventh grade, so I attended several Bar Mitzvah parties. In May, when it became my turn, I gave my mom a list of the kids I wanted to invite. The invitations went out, and the responses began to trickle in. As the RSVP date passed, there were two girls on my list who had not responded. In order to have an accurate count for food and table settings, my mom asked me to call them. Call them? Are you kidding me? These are two of the coolest girls in the school. I can't pick up the phone and call them. Mom insisted, so I eventually complied. What I was told solidified my position in the nerd class and severely damaged my self-esteem, or at least the little bit that I had. These cool girls asked me if I invited the cool boys. Of course, the answer was no. So, the cool girls said they could not come to my party. If the cool boys weren't coming, then neither were they. So, I enjoyed my party with one table of nerdy friends and I even got up the nerve to dance with one of them, the same one who knew French back in the fifth grade. The moment was recorded on film for posterity.

Chapter Seven
High School

The beginning of high school was surprisingly easy for me. Considering my nervousness about going to junior high school and my need to sit in the bathroom for an hour every morning before school, I figured I would be a basket case before my first day of tenth grade. I guess I grew up a little bit.

My high school was 0.8 miles from my house, or about a fifteen-minute walk. At first, it seemed very far away since my elementary school and junior high school were both within sight from my house. By the time I entered the hallowed halls of the school, I suppose I had outgrown some of the bathroom quirks from junior high school. I no longer had to sit in the bathroom for an hour before school, but I was still not too keen on the idea of using the boys' bathroom.

My brother graduated from the same high school six years prior to my first year, so I was somewhat familiar with the school. Some of the teachers remembered him, and I had the advantage of being known as his little brother. Two of my teachers were my brother's classmates, so that helped me get acclimated as well.

Tenth grade was another year of adjustments. Kids were coming together from two different junior high schools and had to get to know each other. I was fortunate that I knew several kids from summer band or little league baseball. It was also a time marked by racial tension following on the heels of the Detroit riots of 1967. In my first year in high school, there was a race riot marked by rock throwing and fighting. Chairs were thrown through the cafeteria windows and kids were fighting on the athletic field. I took refuge in the theater until school was dismissed. That was the only incident of its kind, but the racial tension remained. As in junior high school, there were not very many black students in my classes, and I didn't know any black students very well. I learned from my father's experiences with some of the black employees who worked for him that they didn't work hard and couldn't be trusted. I was actually afraid of some of the black kids in school. It was interesting to me that one of my teachers was a young black man who had grown up in the Township and was a graduate of my high school. He went on to college, played football, played in the band, and majored in mathematics. He was my calculus teacher and one of my favorite people. I never spoke to him about his experiences growing up, but I looked at him as quite the exception. For the most part, the black students I had seen were not good students and did not behave well. I was shocked to see black students in college who were intelligent, talented, and studious. I found that I had a lot to learn about the world.

I had a number of advanced classes, so some of my classmates were juniors and even seniors. I thought it was pretty cool to be in advanced classes. I also felt that I was smarter than these older kids who were in my classes. I was on track to take the most advanced classes offered at the school, and I was proud of myself for that.

I continued to excel in music. Our band was small and not very good so I was able to experiment with other instruments such as the saxophone, bass clarinet, oboe, and the trumpet. I would often play trumpet in the marching band and at basketball games. I really enjoyed the power of the brass instrument. I learned the tenor saxophone well enough to be the lead tenor in our dance band. For some reason, the dance band was very popular, and we had "groupies" who loved to hang around while we played. We all wore very gaudy sport coats and had a great time playing blues and jazz music. Since the choir rehearsals conflicted with band rehearsals, I gave up choir and singing, but I enjoyed hanging around the choir room since many of the girls I liked were there.

I didn't like gym class, especially since I didn't know how to ice skate or swim as we spent time at the rink and in the pool. I did okay on skates and learned how to cross over and snowplow stop. Swimming was another story all together. On our last day in the pool, we had to swim around the perimeter of the pool, including the deep end, without touching the bottom or holding on to the sides for an entire class period. After creating a whirlpool in one direction, we had to reverse our direction. I felt like a salmon trying to swim upstream as I was forcibly sent backward in the water.

In tenth grade, some of my friends were getting involved in homecoming activities and one of them convinced me to show up. The kids were working on the homecoming float and I enjoyed going to someone's house after school to be involved. I made some friends and our class sponsor was an English teacher who happened to be my brother's classmate when they were in high school. Later in the year, the class was going to hold elections for junior class officers. One of my friends was running for president and he asked me to run for an office. I decided to do it and chose to run for vice president. My opponent was a girl who was very popular and very well known to most of the class. I didn't think I had a chance in the world to defeat her, but I gave it a try. I put up some campaign signs around the school, but I lost the election. I was disappointed, but I really didn't have a chance. After the election, the class sponsor came up to me and told me that she hoped I would stay involved in the class activities because I was a great kid. I told her I would be back next school year.

My junior year was a remarkable year. Our class

upset the senior class by winning the spirit award at homecoming. I was dating a cheerleader, doing well in classes, and feeling good about myself. When the class elections were coming up, there was a vacancy for the treasurer position. I decided to run for it and thought I would have a good chance to win, until I found out who would be running against me. My opponent was a girl whom I had known since elementary school. She was athletic, popular, pretty, and I was sure I could not beat her. As the election drew near, several friends came over to my house for a campaign rally. We made signs, buttons, and handouts. My best friend was calling himself my campaign manager, and we had a great time. On the day of the election, I was preparing myself to be disappointed. To my great surprise, I was elected to be the class treasurer. Interestingly enough, when I met my opponent after the election, she told me that she was not surprised at all that I won since I had been so involved and done so much for the class. I actually think she thought I was more popular than she was. Imagine that!

As treasurer, I handled the cash and records for the class. We had some money in a school account as well as petty cash, which I kept at my house. One day in the summer, the class president called to say he was coming over to get some of the money to purchase some needed supplies. When he arrived, I went to the drawer in my bedroom where I kept the money only to find that most of it was gone. I was shocked and started rifling through the drawer to look for the missing money. It was nowhere to be found, so I called to my mom. I told her that the money belonging to the class was gone and my friend was here to pick it up. I didn't know what to do, and I was obviously bothered by the situation. My mom told me that she was short on cash one day, so she took the money. She said that she would write a check and give it to my friend. He was fine with that, but I wasn't. I was angry at my mom for taking the money and for not telling me about it. It was not about the money. It was about my embarrassment in front of my friend. I yelled at my mom, asking her how she could take the money without telling me and that it was my responsibility to keep the money safe. She tried to calm me down and said she would take care of it by writing a check. That didn't matter to me. I was just totally embarrassed in front of my friend and felt irresponsible. No matter what my mom or my friend said to try to calm me down, it was to no avail. I was furious. My mother felt like I was accusing her of thievery and that I didn't trust her. She told me to go hang myself and I went running to my room, slammed the door, flopped onto my bed, and cried my eyes out. How could she not understand my point of view, my embarrassment in front of my friend? How could she take the money without telling me? How could I look so incompetent in front of my friend? How could she tell me to hang myself?

I don't think we said a word to each other for the rest of the day. The following day, my parents and I drove from Michigan to Maryland to visit my aunt. My dad drove, my mom sat in the passenger seat, and I rode in the rear. Hours passed with hardly a word spoken. Neither my mom nor I ever said a word to each other about the incident. I never apologized, nor did I ever try to explain my point of view. Mom never apologized either. The entire incident just went away. I don't know if my mom remembered it later in her life, but it was etched in my memory forever.

High school marked the beginning of my experiences with dating. In tenth grade, my friends would often go out together in small groups. There were some couples who were dating and some who were just part of the group. At first, I was one of the latter. Sometimes, I would ask someone if she would go with me, not as a date, but just in a casual way. There were two sisters who would usually say yes when I would ask either of them, but I never actually dated either one of them. The group would typically go to a movie and then to one of our favorite restaurants for ice cream. It was on one of these group outings that I began my first dating relationship. We went to the movies to see *2001: A Space Odyssey*. I had asked Sally (one of the sisters) to go with me. My best friend, Sam, was dating a girl named Terry, and she was with him. Terry was from the other junior high school and I didn't know her well. I knew she sang in the choir with Sam, but that was about it. The movie was long and there was an intermission. During the intermission, Terry came over to chat with me and she sat on my lap. I didn't know what was going on, but it was clear that she was being flirtatious. I could tell that Sam was getting upset, but I didn't know how to handle this. Soon after this outing, Sam and Terry broke up, and I started dating her. We didn't date for very long when I decided to break up with her. I had asked her to go to a square dance that was part of a Jewish youth group event that many of my friends were attending. She said yes, but then called me later to ask me if this was meant to be a date. I said yes, to which she replied that she didn't want to go with me on a date because she would know so many other boys there. I didn't understand this since it was obvious to me that she would be dancing with other boys. That's what happens at a square dance. At any rate, she pissed me off and I decided to break up with her. I never actually told her that I wanted to break up. I just stopped talking to her. I took the easy way out. After all, I had never broken up with anyone before and was afraid of what might happen. So, I avoided it. And that's how I would do it in the future.

While dating Terry, I met a close friend of hers named Marlene. She was also in the choir and was involved in many of the homecoming activities with me in the eleventh grade. We hit it off well and started dating. Her parents were of Hungarian descent as were mine, so they liked me quite a bit. My parents were very fond of Marlene as well. Marlene and I dated for a few months until I made a mistake. It was a little mistake but, to me, it caused the end of our relationship. Sam asked me if I wanted to double-date with him and his girlfriend to see *1776* at the Midtown Theater. I said yes and, one day, we drove into the city to get tickets. Somehow, we couldn't figure out where the theater was, although it was in a tall building that said General Motors that you could see from a mile away. We ended up driving home, ticketless. That evening, over the phone, I told Marlene the funny story about not finding the theater. She asked me why I would go to get tickets without asking her if she was able to go or wanted to go. She said that I should not have assumed that she could go. (Interestingly enough, neither one of us could have gone that night.) I believed that I had made a fatal error. Rather than apologizing for not asking her first, I put my tail between my legs and shuffled off like a hurt puppy. Because of this mistake, I could no longer speak to Marlene again. No more phone calls in the evening, no more talking and walking together in school, no more dating. I assumed that she didn't want to talk with me anymore, so that's how I left it. We rarely spoke to each other for a year, and neither one of us dated either. I really wanted to get back together, but I was too afraid to speak to her about it. I was hoping that our friends would try to get us back together, but that didn't happen. One night, during the fall of our senior year, we were working with our friends on our senior class homecoming float. Around dinner time, we decided to go out to eat. The consensus was to get ice cream, but Marlene said she would prefer going to her favorite deli. That sounded good to me, so I said I would go with her. I had no ulterior motive about getting back together. I just really wanted a corned beef sandwich. So, we went to the deli, and it was as if we had never been apart. We talked and laughed, but we said nothing about what had happened over the past year. I started talking to her again, calling her, and we resumed dating. We went to senior prom together and continued to date through the summer until we went to different universities. We mutually decided to break up and see what college would bring.

While I was dating Marlene, I was still quite naïve. I know some of my friends were making out, or perhaps doing more than that, and one of my good friends was often teased for being "slow" with the girls. I'm sure I was slower than he was. I would hold Marlene's hand and kiss her goodnight after a date, but that was it. In fact, at our after-the-prom hayride, I was one of the last boys to stop talking and start kissing. I was quite surprised at how Marlene kissed me back. So, this must be what making out is. I was eighteen years old and knew nothing.

Chapter Eight
College Days

Ever since my brother began his college education, my dream was to attend the University of Michigan like he did. His freshman year was in 1964 when I was ten years old. Although it took less than an hour, the trip to Ann Arbor seemed like light years from Oak Park. For our family trips to visit him on Sundays, my father insisted on having a full tank of gas, leaving pretty early in the morning so we could spend some time with him and be able to get home before dark. My father only knew one route to Ann Arbor and, even if there were shorter ways to get there, for us it was always I-94 to State Street. I became a big Wolverine football fan and I was ecstatic when Michigan won the Rose Bowl on New Year's Day 1965 over Oregon State. I had been to a Michigan game that year and fell in love with the maize and blue and the winged helmets. When my brother pledged a fraternity, I wrote the Greek letters on practically everything I owned. My book covers, my box of crayons, my loose leaf, all proudly displayed the three Greek letters. When I started playing clarinet in the band during fifth grade, our songbook had "The Victors," which is Michigan's famous fight song and, although it was toward the back of the book, I learned it as soon as I could. It was in a very low octave on the clarinet and it required using fingerings which we would not learn for a while, but I just had to play it.

As I progressed through school, I was convinced that Michigan was the only school for me. My feeling was that there were only three real options. Michigan is where the smart kids go. Michigan State is where the not-so-smart kids go. Wayne State is where everyone else goes, especially if they want to live at home. I applied only to Michigan since I was pretty sure I would be accepted and I really didn't want to go anywhere else. When I got accepted to Michigan, I was thrilled and I went out and bought Michigan T-shirts to wear to school. I even found a pair of yellow-and-blue suede shoes that I just had to have. They were pretty atrocious, but I thought they were beautiful and I wore them proudly. I believe the last time I wore them was at Michigan during a very wet and rainy marching band practice that left my feet yellow and blue as well.

During the summer before my first semester at Michigan, I attended orientation. When I arrived, I checked in to my room and met my roommate. I didn't know him and my only recollection of him was that he had long hair and was rolling joints, something I was completely unfamiliar with. While I was at orientation, my longtime friend and soon-to-be freshman roommate Sam arrived to begin his orientation. I was happy to have him there since I was shy about meeting other people. I had a car, so we drove around Ann Arbor for a while then retired to our dorm rooms. While some kids were getting high, partying, and doing whatever they felt like during their brief stay on campus, I pretty much did nothing. On the last day of orientation, it was time to register for my first semester of college courses. In high school, I was generally a math and science kid. I had very little interest in history or government. I didn't enjoy reading books and I hated writing papers (although somehow I got advanced placement credit in English so I didn't have to take an English class). I didn't feel like taking any more math and science, and the course catalog was huge and intimidating.

I had no idea what my major would be or what I wanted to do for a career. Feeling lost, I sought out the help of my brother. He helped me understand the graduation requirements for the College of Literature, Science, and the Arts (LS&A), which is where most students land unless they want to go into a specific field such as engineering or business. In order to graduate, I would have to accumulate many hours in humanities, social science, natural science, and whatever my major would be. It was not unusual for a freshman to be uncertain about a major field, so the only thing I needed to concern myself with was taking classes that sounded interesting to me that would begin to fulfill the requirements. So, my brother and I talked about the types of classes that freshmen take and from our discussion, I made my selections. Marching band was a given. I was eager to devote a great deal of my time and energy for one lousy credit, a forty-dollar band award, the opportunity to wear a Michigan Band jacket (which I did pretty much every day), and the thrill of performing with one of the best marching bands in the country. My other choices were political science (I hated it), sociology (I tolerated it), Russian (which I took just for fun and loved it), and anthropology (boring). In my second semester, I took my first psychology class. I signed up for the class because a girl I had a major crush on told me that we should take it together. We didn't have a psychology class in high school, so this was my first exposure to the subject. I was fascinated by the things we read and the research that was being conducted. We visited the Kresge Hearing Research Institute Laboratories on campus, where I learned about experiments being done to determine effects of drugs and medications on hearing. I was hooked and decided that psychology would be my major, although I was not required to declare a major field of study until my junior year.

I took several psychology courses to fulfill my major and was doing quite well in school. I was never going to be a straight-A student because I didn't work that hard. But my grades were more than respectable. As a junior, I applied for entrance into the honors psychology program and was accepted. Being accepted into this program simply meant that I was allowed to take a class with other honor students. When I received the letter of acceptance, I had a giant rush of low self-esteem. I couldn't believe that I was actually accepted (this would be a common theme in my life). I was rooming with several quirky guys that year and I told one of them that I got accepted, but I didn't know why. This led to one of my roommates writing a cute little song about me, which pretty much describes how I viewed myself. There was a song called "Shaving Cream" that was written by Benny Bell in 1946. It is a silly little song where it sounds like each verse is going to end with the word "shit" but it is replaced with "Shaving Cream" and it starts all over again. For example, my ham sandwich tasted like shhhh . . . aving cream.

The song was being played on the Dr. Demento radio show in the 1970s. Vanguard Records reissued the song in 1975 and became a hit, peaking at number thirty on the Billboard Hot 100 chart. It was often heard on Ann Arbor radio stations and my clever roommate came up with a version for me, which I heard many times. It went like this:

"Gray's grades in psychology were high
This troubled him quite a bit
He said but, but I don't know why

> I thought my performance was . . . shhhhh
> . . . aving cream,
> be nice and clean. . . .
> Shave ev'ry day and you'll always look
> keen."

Although the song was meant to be a joke, it was a serious indicator of my view of self-worth and my ability to give myself credit. The honors psychology class turned out to be a painful experience for me. It was a small class of perhaps no more than ten students. The class was led by a graduate assistant and was very informal. On nice days, we would meet outside to enjoy the weather and relax while sitting on the ground near some trees. I still had no idea what I wanted to do with my life and, of course, I assumed that all of the other students had a plan in place for graduate school, career, and ultimate fame and fortune. I never spoke to anyone in the class, and I never said a word about any of the articles we read. It was not because I was unprepared. I had read all the articles prior to our classes. I just felt like anything I had to say would be wrong or might lead to a debate, and I would never be able to debate with any of these honor students. The only thing I ever contributed was the name of the author of *A Room with a View*. No one could remember the author's name and somehow I did, although I had never read the book. I was not much of a reader. When I uttered "E. M. Forster," everyone suddenly glanced at the previously silent human being to see whose voice this was. I felt really stupid that this was all I would say, but I got an A in the class for doing the required assignments. Ironically, one of the students married someone whom my wife's family knew, so I got to see her on a few occasions. The girl who had been in my class didn't strike me as impressive, even though she was once an intimidating honors psychology student.

During study days at the end of my junior year at Michigan, I started thinking about my future. I pictured myself graduating with a degree in psychology, going on to a graduate degree in psychology, and pursuing a PhD. I was interested in experimental psychology as opposed to clinical psychology. I saw myself as a professor of some kind who wore a white coat and worked in a laboratory running rats through mazes. It's not that this life didn't appeal to me but I was now in a relationship with Lauren and, although we had only been dating for a few months, I felt strongly that we might get married someday. I started having thoughts about making a living and having a job. I started wondering how I would be able to make a living and support a family. I sat in the cubicle in the undergraduate library and felt scared and panicky. I couldn't concentrate on my studies at all. I felt the urge to escape. The fun and games of college life were over as I considered the onset of adulthood. I couldn't find Lauren, so I told her friend Angela to let her know that I was going

home. Angela and Lauren assumed I meant back
to my apartment. I meant I was going home to my
parents' home. I felt lost and confused. Without
considering talking to Lauren, some of my
professors, or an academic counselor, I bolted from
the library and drove home.

I talked to my mom about my concerns. I can't
remember the conversation, but I remember that
Time Magazine had a cover story about the MBA.
The master's in business administration was the
ticket. Corporations were looking to hire MBAs,
especially from the best schools. Without much
thought or information, I decided that the best
thing for me would be to complete my degree in
psychology and to take classes during my senior
year that were required for admission to the MBA
program. Since I was good at mathematics, I
assumed that I would enjoy accounting and being
a CPA sounded like a career that would be
profitable. So during my senior year, I took an
economics course, a calculus course (which was
very easy since they used the same textbook I had
used in high school), and an accounting course, to
see if I liked it. During the summer before I started
my MBA program, I took a second accounting
course. To my dismay, I discovered that accounting and mathematics are not the same. I hated
accounting. But the die was cast and I was on my
way to Michigan Business School for the next two
years to get my MBA.

My acceptance to Michigan Business School

was consistent with other accomplishments in my life. I never expected it to happen, and I didn't believe it when it did. I was graduating with a BA in psychology with a respectable GPA of 3.1. Not bad, but I assumed not good enough for Michigan, which was probably in the top five programs in the country. I wanted to stay in Ann Arbor, but I was thinking that my odds were slim. I applied to six graduate programs, all within the state of Michigan. I didn't know much about any of them, but I wanted to remain close to home and to Lauren, who would be in Ann Arbor for at least another year. I took my Graduate Management Admission Test (GMAT) and I did pretty well. I still didn't think my scores would be up to Michigan standards, so I took them again. My applications had been submitted and now I just had to wait. I received a phone call from one of the schools telling me that I had been accepted and they wanted to talk with me about my plans. I told them that I wasn't ready to commit yet since I was waiting to hear from Michigan. I was happy to know that I had a place to go, but I wanted Michigan. One spring day, I arrived at my apartment after class and was greeted by my roommate Sam who said, "Gray, you got into Michigan Business School." He handed me a package which had arrived in the mail. I told him that it might not be an acceptance, but he said that one of our friends got the same size package and he was accepted. I tore it open and found it to be

Robert Gray

true. I had been accepted to the MBA program at Michigan. I immediately called Lauren, who lived only a couple of blocks away in a sorority house, and she rushed over to my apartment. We both were happy and relieved to know that we would be together in Ann Arbor for at least another year. It was a wonderful feeling to be in love and to know that the future was starting to come into focus. The next two years of business school were stressful for me, to say the least. It provided me with many chances to feel inferior, experience anxiety, and question my abilities. I came out bruised and battered but I had a graduate degree, a job, a wife, and a life ahead of me.

Chapter Nine
B School

During the summer after graduation, I took my second accounting class. I didn't really like the first one very much, but I was stubborn and tried again. This class was taught by a young graduate student with a very heavy Chinese accent. Many of the students had difficulty understanding him, but we did the best we could. This second class confirmed for me that I didn't like accounting. However, after taking the two classes, I decided to take an exam to try to place out of first-year accounting in business school. I took the exam and didn't pass it. Shortly after, I learned something about Lauren's father, Harvey, the hard way.

Lauren and I were visiting her parents' home one summer evening when Harvey asked me if I had passed the accounting exam. I told him that I did not and, in his deep, gravelly, and gruff voice, he replied, "Why not?" I stammered something about not being prepared and shuffled off in embarrassment. I don't think I said another word all evening, and the drive back to Ann Arbor with Lauren was almost silent. The odometer on my little yellow station wagon was going to change to fifty thousand miles and I told her that it was about to change. That was the only thing I said during the entire drive. The two of us also ignored the fact that an electric cord from a table fan, which we were taking to school, was dangling out the back door, making noise as it scraped along the pavement. I don't know what Lauren was thinking during the ride home, but she let me sit in my silence. When we arrived at her sorority house, we sat on the stairs and talked. She told me that her father meant nothing by his comment and was not upset that I didn't pass. That is just how he is and what he sounds like. She told me that if I couldn't learn to deal with his personality, then we would not have much a future together. I broke down and sobbed in her arms, feeling like a wounded little boy. The anxiety about going to business school was starting to show itself, but I didn't want to admit that to anyone.

Before classes started, I had an opportunity to go to an orientation where I met some of the professors and students. Having a degree in psychology and knowing that accounting was not in the cards for me, I chatted with one of the professors about organizational behavior and industrial relations. He told me that some psychology majors find that field to be interesting. I stayed for a short while before returning to my room in an old house on campus. My takeaways from the orientation were that there were many older students who had work experience, there were many students from other countries who came to Michigan and would return to their home country with a valuable MBA, and there were many students who looked very comfortable in the environment. I didn't notice anyone else shaking in their boots.

The night before the first day of class, I thought I was dying. I lay on my bed feeling anxiety. I was cold and shaking and I thought I was having a heart attack. I called Lauren, but she told me to relax and that I would be fine. I went to class on the first day and found out that it was not as terrible as I had expected. There were some students who looked like I could get along with. Not everyone was intimidating. Some of them came from liberal arts backgrounds. Some of them did not have work experience. There were even a couple of goofy kids who looked like they just wanted to have fun. I managed to find my clique and didn't speak much to other students.

The biggest worry for me about business school was class participation. In most classes, the professor would call on a student to begin class discussion based on a case study we had prepared. He would carry the seating chart with him and make marks to indicate who spoke and the quality of their answer. Since I hated being wrong and embarrassed, I was usually nervous at the beginning of class. Once the first student was called on, I would settle down a bit. But I usually didn't have much to say. On one occasion in my finance class, I was sitting in the back row of the

Robert Gray

small auditorium where I was helping a fellow student with a computer program for another class. The professor was lecturing and writing something on the board, but my attention was focused on the program. Suddenly, I heard my name being called from the front of the room. The professor, who obviously saw that I was not paying attention, called on me to answer a question. I was so scared and I asked him to repeat the question. The question was not a difficult one and, based on what he had written on the board, I had a fifty-fifty chance at being right. But at the time, I stared at the board and to me it looked like some language which I didn't understand. He asked me again for an answer, but I just sat in silence as a hush spread around the room. I felt that the students all turned to stare at me with derision, thinking I must be such an idiot. The professor finally let me off the hook and called on another student, while making a mark on his seating chart by my name. I believed that every student would think of me as a dummy. That would be appropriate since that's what I thought of myself.

I was never very willing to have conversations with my professors. They intimidated me and I never thought they would want to talk to me, even though they were supposed to be available to the students. There was an occasion where my fear of getting called on in class outweighed my fear of professors. One night, I struggled with an assignment and just did not understand how to do the problems. Since I didn't have many friends and I was too stubborn to ask for help anyway, I decided to go to the professor early in the morning prior to class and beg him not to call on me. He was in his office that morning and I told him that I didn't understand the assignment. I asked him not to call on me and he said that most students would not understand this assignment so he would be going over it in class. I was relieved to know that the pressure was off, but the part about other students not getting it did not sink in. I still felt like this lowly psychology major and former marching bandsman couldn't possibly measure up to the students who were on their way to one of the big marketing companies or one of the large accounting or financial institutions.

Lauren and I got married a few weeks before my final year in the MBA program. We moved into a small apartment in married housing and began our lives together. For some reason, this had a calming effect on me. I was no longer eating antacids every day, although I bought a large bottle before school started. The biggest focus during the second year of business school is getting a job. Students would wear their suits to school quite often to interview with the many companies that came to Michigan to recruit. Finishing the program was a foregone conclusion for most of us, so I suppose the pressure was off. I signed up for several interviews, but I didn't really want to move away from Michigan. One of my best

Robert Gray

interviews was with the telephone company. I recognized the recruiter, who was an athlete at Michigan State University and a member of the Oakland A's championship team in 1974. He was a sprinter and the A's used him to do nothing but steal bases. In his two years with the A's he appeared in 105 regular season games and 5 post-season games never having an at-bat. He wore a very noticeable World Series ring, and I used my knowledge of sports and my rivalry with Michigan State to reduce my stress. It worked and in February, with over two months to graduation, I had accepted a job offer to do marketing research in Detroit. It was perfect for us since we could be close to our parents and families. My friends in school were very happy for me and wished me well. But, in typical business school form, one of my fellow students came up to me and said, "Did you really want to take that job at the telephone company or did you take it because you thought you wouldn't get anything better?" I walked away without dignifying his question with a response. But it made me feel like I had enough of this place and I was looking forward to moving on. To this day, I have never attended a graduate function at the school and I have not been in contact with anyone from the program. After enjoying four years at Michigan as an undergraduate student, my two years as a graduate student were a living hell. Of course, I did my best to hide it.

Chapter Ten
Perfection

I was one of those people who hated being wrong. Getting a bad grade on a test or quiz was not something that happened to me very often. But, when it did, it was devastating and a major blow to my self-worth. I took all of the advanced classes that were available in junior high school and high school. I chose to take French over Spanish since most of the "smart" kids took French. My parents never had to tell me to do my homework since being unprepared in a class was something I had trouble dealing with. I wasn't always the best and I didn't have a 4.0 average, but I was always one of the best. In the eighth grade, I had trouble with geometry, but I worked very hard to understand it and to improve my grade before the end of the semester. In addition to my fear of being wrong, I also had a fear of asking for help. By asking for help, I was admitting that I couldn't do it myself and that was as embarrassing as being wrong. This led me to many hours of unnecessary frustration and worry since I would struggle to get it on my own rather than have someone explain it to me. And I hated being unprepared in class, so, on those days when I didn't understand, I would pray that I wouldn't be called on. Of course, I assumed that I was the only one who didn't understand and I would be singled out as an idiot. In my junior year of high school, I took an advanced mathematics class which met in the afternoon after lunch. Many of my friends had the same class, with the same teacher, in the morning. The teacher always called students to the board to write out the solution to one of the homework problems. If there was a problem which I couldn't do, I would get together at lunch with my friends from the morning class and copy their solution into my notebook. If I got called to the board, I would be able to do the problem. I did anything to avoid the embarrassment of admitting that I didn't have the solution. This teacher was also known for collecting our notebooks to check other assigned problems. So, I also had to make sure that my notebook was complete. Bear in mind that I was not the only afternoon-class student who participated in this lunchtime activity, but that didn't mean anything to me. All I knew was that, if I didn't know the answer or was unprepared, the entire school would be talking about it because I was so special.

I was not the greatest student when it came to chemistry. Lab work was a cinch, but I had trouble with theory and balancing equations. Asking the teacher for help was, of course, out of the question, so I did all I could on my own. One day, the teacher, Mr. Newton, who was also one of the football coach, handed out a pop quiz. We all put our books on the floor and began. I remember being confused by the first question, and I got nervous. I couldn't figure it out, so I started looking at the paper of the student to my left. He was not a particularly good student, but I had to do something. I couldn't ask Mr. Newton for clarification or help since that would expose my ignorance. So, I tried to cheat. All of a sudden, I heard my name being called from the front of the room. Mr. Newton saw what I was doing and asked me to hand in my quiz. I was going to get a zero for trying to cheat. I handed in my quiz and returned to my desk, where I slumped down in shame. I said nothing to my parents about this. I assumed once again that the whole school would be talking about how I got caught cheating and how stupid I was. I expected that kids would tease me endlessly and that there would be an article in the school newspaper about my indiscretion. Of course, nobody cared, nobody said anything to me about it, and the earth kept turning. But the effect on me was long-lasting. I avoided Mr. Newton at all costs, assuming that he didn't like me or respect me. He was one of the more popular teachers in the school, but I wanted nothing to do with him. I was afraid to apologize or admit that I had made a mistake by trying to cheat. Maybe if I didn't bring it up, it would just go away.

One day, near the end of the semester, Mr. Newton called us up one at a time to look at our grades. He said that he was dropping our lowest quiz or test grade. I assumed that he was going to make me keep the zero to punish me. I sat nervously awaiting my turn as if I was going to walk *The Green Mile* to Old Sparky. He called me to the front of the room. Since my cheating incident, I had not said a single word to him and I had no idea what to expect. He showed me my grades in his grade book, pointed to the zero, and said that, of course, we would drop that one. I was so relieved and I returned to my desk. I think I got a C for the class but I was grateful for it. Because all of my friends were going to take the chemistry laboratory course the following year, I registered for it too. After all, that was what was expected of all of the smart kids. On the day of registration at the school, my brother showed up unexpectedly. He told me that my mother was concerned about me taking another chemistry class after my performance in the first one. He suggested taking Spanish instead. After all, why would I ever need chemistry later in life? Adding Spanish to my French classes would help me more in the future. I felt embarrassed that he came to school. I didn't need my older brother to tell me what to do. Nobody else's older brother showed up to give their siblings advice. Besides, dropping chemistry and taking Spanish would mean I was not worthy of being on the advanced track with the best of the best. What would everyone think if I didn't take classes with all of the smartest kids? I don't remember what I said to my brother, but I'm sure it was not complimentary. I took the chemistry class and got an A. The lab work was fun and interesting for me. The class was taught by the same teacher, Mr. Newton, and I still had very little to do with him. As a matter of fact, he had me confused with another student and often called me Joey. I was so shy and insecure that I let him call me Joey for most of the year. It was only toward the end of the term that I actually corrected him. Most of the students in the class liked Mr. Newton, but I could not approach him after the cheating incident. He probably didn't even remember my cheating crime from the year before. I was probably not the only student he ever caught cheating. But it has remained in my memory for almost five decades.

Chapter Eleven
Girls, Women, and Sex

My knowledge and understanding of sex was obtained in elementary school. My parents and I didn't have conversations about things like that, so I depended on teachers in elementary school to learn about it. I discovered masturbation around the age of fifteen and found it to be a pleasurable experience. I heard boys talk about it in school, but I never said anything at all. I didn't want anyone to know that I was doing it and get teased about it. Of course, I assumed that I was the only one who was indulging in masturbation. I never told my parents about it because, as I said, we just didn't talk about things like that. Like most boys, I had my share of encounters with *Playboy* Magazine and centerfold jigsaw puzzles were all the rage when I was in high school. I believed that many of the kids in my high school were sexually active, but I sure wasn't one of them.

I had very few casual dates and, in my years as a single young man, I had a grand total of four girlfriends, two in high school and two in college. I only liked dating one girl at a time and I expected my girlfriend to only date me. But, while I was dating in high school, I was friendly with many of the girls in my class through involvement in class activities. Although I didn't date most of them, I would often write them letters which I would deliver to their homes very late at night. I was too shy to call them on the phone or to ask them out, so this became my way of communicating. Girls thought this was cute and started calling me the Midnight Mailman. Some would even ask if they could expect a letter from me some night, and many wrote comments in my yearbook about the letters. Sometimes I would write several letters in one night. Sometimes I would have more to say to a girl whom I wasn't dating than I would to the girl I was dating. Perhaps this behavior was fore-shadowing what was to happen in the future.

The thought of having sexual intercourse before marriage was interesting to me, but I didn't have the courage to ever even talk about it. I wasn't even sure that I knew how to do it, and I certainly didn't want to embarrass myself. I was well aware that many of my college friends were doing it, but I was not. I was painfully shy and there were many girls that I was attracted to or interested in, but I wouldn't even ask them out. I was extremely fortunate that when I met Lauren for the first time, she invited me to a party at her sorority the next night, and then she called me later in the week to ask me if I wanted to go out. I had actually gotten sick the day after the sorority house party and basically lost my nerve to call her. Had she not called me, who knows where my life would have ended up?

Although I had very few girlfriends, I usually had many friends, or at least acquaintances who were girls. I was generally well liked in spite of my own perceived shortcomings. I enjoyed making girls laugh and I liked being flirtatious. I felt intimidated by many of the more athletic, macho guys and I felt more comfortable with girls. Even when I was dating Lauren, I would often go to hockey games with some of her sorority sisters. Lauren didn't like hockey and the girls didn't want to go alone, so it just made sense. I also spent many hours in the sorority house, even when Lauren wasn't there. I would often study there or just chitchat with some of the girls. I found some of the girls to be attractive and, although I was in a relationship with Lauren, I didn't feel this was unusual or wrong. After we were married, I still didn't feel that finding other women to be attractive was unusual or wrong, but sometimes my feelings would become too strong.

Throughout my teens and early adult years, I enjoyed imagining fantasies with women and masturbation even while I was dating and after marriage. I thought many times that I should stop and I often tried to abstain from it, but I was never able to. Like most people, I found the experience to be pleasurable, so I kept doing it. Many sources indicate that masturbation is normal whether you are in a sexual relationship or not, and there are even benefits to masturbation. Although statistics show that most men masturbate, I still thought that there was something unusual about me. But, when I had to masturbate into a cup for infertility tests and artificial insemination, it was no big deal to me. And, my eventual experiences into cybersex gave me another way to create scenarios for pleasure.

In my first year out of graduate school, there was an attractive woman in my department at work who told me that she was in fact married to one of the men in the group. She had been using her maiden name and keeping her relationship a secret. So, before they decided to go public with the fact that they were married, she came to tell me so I wouldn't be surprised. I remember feeling sad that she was no longer available. Available for what? I had been married for over a year. What was I thinking? Two years later, I found myself enamored with another young woman at work. I enjoyed her personality and we hit it off well. One night, when Lauren was going to school at night, I met this woman for dinner. It wasn't a date, but we had dinner together. It was usually difficult to find time during the day to have lunch together, so we had to meet for dinner. She was also married. She began to shy away from me when she realized that I had feelings for her, and nothing ever came of it. I would never have had the nerve to continue in a relationship with her, but there was a definite feeling of excitement in the fantasy. Several years later, I worked on a project which required me to be out of town for several weeks. Once again, I met a young woman to whom I was attracted. After seeing her every day for three weeks, I actually felt like I was falling in love with her. I confided in one of my friends about my feelings and cried as I told him what was going on in my head. I told him that it was wrong of me to have these feelings and that I was so confused by them. I knew nothing would ever happen with her and that I would never see her again, but having such strong feelings for her scared me. As far as I was concerned, things like this were not right and were not supposed to happen to me. But right or wrong, they were happening to me, I was having these feelings, and unbeknownst to me, my world would crash down upon me six years later because of it.

It is certainly not unusual for a married man to be attracted to a woman. Being attracted is one thing, but developing strong feelings is another. I could have sought counseling to talk about these feelings. I could have opened up to Lauren to tell her that perhaps we needed marital counseling to figure out why this was happening to me. Perhaps I could have prevented my misadventures in cyberspace if I would have said something. But no. I kept everything bottled up inside me. I kept my deep, dark secrets because I was afraid to face a problem head on. I suffered in silence again. And I came so very close to completely destroying my family and my life.

Chapter Twelve
The Shame of Infertility

After Lauren and I were married, we lived in married housing while I finished my graduate studies. After graduation, we lived in a couple of apartments until we bought our first house. Having a place of our own, we decided it was time to start a family. Soon, we were excited to be expecting our first child. Unfortunately, it was an ectopic pregnancy and it didn't last. We were lucky that Lauren was fine and that we would be able to continue to try to have a baby with no complications. After several months with no success, Lauren's doctor suggested a sperm test to see if there were any issues. I remember the afternoon of that day as if it were yesterday. I was shooting baskets at the hoop on our garage when Lauren arrived home from work. She told me that the test results were back. She said that my sperm count was about four million. Having no idea what a typical sperm count should be, that sounded like a pretty good number to be. Four million sounds like lots of little swimmers. But then she told me that the average sperm count is in the neighborhood of fifty to sixty million. My heart sank. My manhood was in question. After having to shower with boys in gym class, I knew that I was

Robert Gray

not blessed with one of the larger organs on the block, which didn't make me feel too good and instead left me embarrassed. I wasn't thinking about the chances of having a baby as much as I was thinking about my own self-esteem and identity. Lauren suggested that I talk to my doctor about it, not only from a medical standpoint, but also from a personal one. His sperm count had been low but he and his wife had been successful having children. I contacted him and he discussed the situation with me. He assured me that this means nothing with respect to virility or manhood and that he understood how I felt. He also told me that he was going to prescribe a medication that might help. It was an estrogen modulator that can treat infertility in men but was usually given to women to regulate their menstrual cycles. There had been some research done to indicate that it could increase the sperm count in males. I thought it was pretty weird to take a female drug, so I asked him about contraindications. The only things listed were possible vaginal pain and breast soreness. Great! All I need is some drug that is going to give me vaginal pain. He assured me that he thought I should try the medication. I took the drug just the way a woman would, twenty days on and five days off. It didn't have a miraculous effect on my sperm count but there were positive results. In 1984, Lauren and I were blessed with our daughter Aline through the use of this medication.

After Aline was born, we relocated to Illinois

and eventually decided it was time to have a second child. New doctors, new tests, new results. My sperm count was still not wonderful but there were also issues with motility and the overall health of the sperm. A visit to a urologist disclosed a new, or perhaps previously undiagnosed, problem. I had varicose veins which meant that some of the blood in my veins was flowing back against the blood flow causing heat from the friction. Heat is not a good thing for sperm, so this situation had to be corrected. The procedure to correct this is a bilateral varicocele ligation. A varicocele is a bundle of enlarged veins in the scrotum. The veins become enlarged because some of the tiny valves inside the veins don't close properly. The valves normally prevent blood from draining backward. When the valves fail, blood pools in the veins, causing them to swell. The extra blood pooling in the enlarged veins warms the nearby testicle unnaturally and cuts sperm production. The solution is to perform surgery to detour the flow of blood into normal veins. After the surgery, we did have one pregnancy but it didn't last. After many months of trying, and several sperm tests, we were referred to an infertility specialist. More tests, more counts, more frustration. I got so accustomed to providing semen samples that I no longer needed the magazines which they so kindly provided.

Lovemaking became an event driven by the calendar rather than love. I felt like if it wasn't the right day for conception then there was no need to waste my little swimmers. It didn't matter if we felt like it or not; the calendar said it's time. Sometimes, I would have to travel for my job and it was traumatic if I had to be gone on one of the lovemaking days. Lauren would get emotional and accuse me of not wanting to have a baby. I would get emotional and tell her that I couldn't control when these trips would occur. We were slaves to her cycle and we were stressed out. Things just weren't working at all and we were ready to try anything. We progressed to the next step, which was artificial insemination. The doctor prescribed a medication, which was to be administered by me through intramuscular injection. I was taught how to give Lauren these injections which were to increase our chances of conception. We were told that the probability of multiple births was also increased but we were willing to take that chance.

The medication was a liquid that came in a small bottle with a scored neck. I'm sure I filled Lauren with confidence as I cut my finger on the bottle when I was being taught how to give her the shot. The injections were to be given in the hip area and I generally did okay with the injections. However, there was one time when I hesitated, inserted the needle too slowly, and Lauren was seeing stars. So now, the act of making love became completely clinical. I didn't even have to be in the same building to make it happen. While Lauren waited for her appointment, I headed for one of the rooms with the comfortable couch and the magazines so I could produce my specimen in the jar. I would put the jar in the little door on the wall, get myself together, exit into the waiting room where I could give Lauren a kiss, and then head off to work. How romantic! We were fortunate that the medication worked after only two months. In July of 1989, we were so blessed to welcome Hilary, Michael, and Eric into the world. Three healthy babies who all came home from the hospital after only five days. All you need is love, along with a calendar, some drugs, and an enormous amount of patience.

Chapter Thirteen
Career

In graduate school, students did not declare a major field of study. However, most of the students concentrated in a particular field to prepare for their careers. I chose to concentrate in marketing. It wasn't so much that I loved marketing but it was the least evil of the choices available to me. The dream of most marketing students was to be a product manager for one of the large consumer-product companies. I had no such desire but I did interview for those jobs since the recruiters were available to us. I liked the marketing research class I took since it involved logic in study, questionnaire design, analysis of data, and making decisions based on the data. Most marketing students were not interested in marketing research jobs since they weren't as glamourous or lucrative. I was happy to accept my first job as an analyst doing marketing as well as employee research studies.

At the telephone company, the organization was called business research and it was housed within the treasury department. It seemed to me to be a strange alignment but it did allow a great deal of objectivity. Our clients were mainly marketing, directory, human resources, and public relations. There were only four analysts in my group and we were mostly young and relatively new to the business. Most of my projects were pretty straightforward. I would get an assignment from my manager and would set up a fact-finding meeting with the client organization. Based on their information needs and study objectives, I would design and implement a plan to obtain the research data and write a report. I found all parts of my job to be enjoyable and I learned quite a bit about the company. The most difficult part of the job was the report writing. My manager, whom we called Jaws (her initials were JAS), was a very difficult person to write for. She had some experience with this type of report writing in a previous job, so she felt she was the expert. My peers used to dread having their reports critiqued and rewritten by Jaws. I can still remember how they would storm out of her office with a look of complete anger. Keep in mind that reports were written by hand in the late 1970s and then typed by a clerical person. Editing and correcting reports took time and often the client was eager for their results. Somehow, I tended to avoid the red pen of Jaws. I was able to figure out how to adapt my writing to her style, so I rarely had difficulties. I do remember one argument I had with her about how to write up a report finding for her former organization. I wrote that 90 percent of the respondents had no recollection of receiving a public relations publication which was sent to them. My boss insisted that I change it to 10 percent of the respondents recalled receiving the publication. I felt that the majority should be reported on but I lost the argument. Rank has its privilege.

After my first year in business research, Jaws asked me where I wanted to go in my career. Within the treasury department, there was not much of a future for me, so I started looking toward marketing. At that time, marketing was mostly sales, so I was pushed in that direction. I was not at all interested in sales but I took the assessment to be an account executive. I told my boss that I wouldn't pass and I was right. I was so analytical during the assessment that I made twenty-eight recommendations from the case study and totally ignored any social cues they were giving me to try to shut me up. So, after two years in marketing research, I moved into a job doing seminars for customers. There was no real reason for me to leave my job but people generally stayed only about two years. I didn't tell anyone that I didn't want to leave and, on the day that I packed up my desk, I sat and cried, wondering why I was leaving a job I liked. I never said a word about this. I just left for the next job.

I moved from the downtown headquarters building to a building in the suburbs. It was a much shorter commute for me but that was the only positive thing I could come up with. My new

position was a customer service representative—
Phone Power. Most of the people in my new group
had sales experience and I felt like the nerdy guy
who had to try to fit in. Phone Power was a program
that was designed to improve a customer's inside
sales, outside sales, and collecting overdue accounts
through more effective use of the telephone. Our
customers were mostly small- to medium-sized
businesses around the state of Michigan. The job
was to conduct seminars with our customers'
employees and to teach them the Phone Power
techniques. The seminars were free of charge, so it
wasn't too difficult to sell free training to them. Our
success was measured in increased telephone usage
and any other equipment or services that they
happened to buy. An increase in telephone usage
often had nothing to do with our seminars and
training but, nevertheless, that was the measurement. For example, I could train a company who
was expanding their workforce, so, naturally, their
telephone usage would increase. It was all about
luck and timing. As an analytical person, I found
this measurement of success to be bogus but I had
to play the game.

Those who work in Phone Power received
training on how to conduct a seminar. When I
started, I didn't come in as part of a group, so there
was no training scheduled for me. So, I sat in on a
couple of seminars run by different people and took
copious notes. I then taught portions of the seminars
with my coworkers and eventually started training

on my own. My coworkers and managers were amazed at how quickly I caught on and how well I could lead a seminar. But to me, it was no different from some of the presentations I had to make in school. I enjoyed teaching and there was an ego rush for me to be in the front of the room and in control. Teaching seemed to be a natural thing for me. I really thought that it was no big deal that I was able to learn the material and speak in front of a seminar audience but my boss and coworkers were amazed. People tell me that they fear public speaking more than dying but, for me, it is easy. This ability would serve me well throughout my career. But, of course, I still think it is no big deal.

I stayed in the Phone Power job for a year but it was a real waste of time. I did well in the job and I learned some things about myself and others. One of the things I learned was something called Social Styles Sales Strategies. I became good at determining the style of the person I was "selling" to and how to adapt my logical, analytical, detailed style to increase the probability of success. On one occasion, my boss accompanied me on a visit to an insurance company. I was to meet with the sales manager of the office and convince him that I should train his people on phone-selling techniques. As we sat and waited for him in his office, my manager asked me to look around and tell her the social style of the sales manager. I took note of many plaques on the wall indicating high achievement. He had many photos of events, golf outings, and team activities. His desk was cluttered and there were papers on the floor. I told my boss that I thought he was an expressive person who was proud of his accomplishments. She asked me how I would alter my approach based on this observation and I told her that I would not use my preprinted flip charts. She nodded in agreement. When the sales manager walked in, he shook our hands, sat down, and said to me, "So, what can you do for me Bob?" I bristled at the sound of the name Bob, since nobody calls me Bob. But I certainly wasn't going to correct him and tell him that I go by the more formal name of Robert. I answered his question with, "I see from the plaque on the wall that your team was number two in the region last year. Congratulations. I am here to make you number one." He rose from his chair, shook my hand enthusiastically, and told me to get started. End of meeting. Yes, I learned how to play the game, but I wasn't cut out for this.

I began an internal job search and I found out that the internal auditing department was hiring, so I went for an interview and was hired. I had no idea what internal auditing was but it sounded interesting. I was trained in procedures, controls, report writing, and documentation. During the training, I found the analytical part of the job to be fun and interesting. The part I didn't like was defending my findings to the auditee and putting them on the spot. Many of the people in the training enjoyed debating and the confrontational nature of the interactions but I felt very uncomfortable with this aspect.

My boss was a stickler for detail and we got along well since I was comfortable working for a detail-oriented person. I generally enjoyed the job since it was intellectually challenging at times. I had to learn a lot quickly, manage my own projects, and write reports. My biggest problem with this job was procrastination. I usually took longer than the assigned number of days to do an audit. Usually, I spent too much time preparing for it since I thought I had to be perfect and know everything before putting a plan together and talking with auditees. Although the auditees were the ones doing the work, I felt I had to know the job better than they did. I had to feel ready before starting my fieldwork and, by that time, I was already behind the eight-ball. But I was promoted during this time, so I must have been doing something right. Similar to my previous business research position, my ability to adapt my writing style to my boss's style was a strength for me. He seemed to have an aversion to prepositional phrases, so I learned to string adjectives together in long strings just to avoid using the words "of" and "from." Rather than writing something like, "Ten service orders were sampled from the Company's Special Service Unit in Southfield," I would write, "Ten Company Southfield Special Service Unit service orders were sampled." I thought it was ridiculous but it wasn't worth arguing about.

The divestiture of the Bell System in 1984
provided me with a choice. I could stay at the
telephone company or take an internal auditing job
with the long-distance telephone company or the
telephone equipment provider in Chicago.
Although my family and my wife's family were in
Michigan, the prospect of living and working in
Chicago appealed to me. We had friends there and
had visited several times. Chicago was such a
vibrant city as compared to Detroit. I had met the
managers of both organizations and learned that
one job was in the city and the other was in the
western suburb of Oak Brook. I thought I liked one
of the managers better and his group was in the
city, so I chose to go with the long-distance
telephone company in Chicago. Traveling on the
suburban train was so cool. I would pick up the
Chicago Tribune to read the sports section and I
would see the city get larger as we approached.
Going home, I felt like I was escaping the hustle
and bustle of the city and coming to the
peacefulness of our little village. I felt like I was in
the mainstream, living in the adult world, like I
had arrived. I only wished that my job provided
me at least an ounce of satisfaction. At divestiture,
many people had no idea what they should be
doing. It was a very confusing time in the
telecommunications industry. The internal
auditing department was on the second floor of a
very nice building in Chicago. The auditors were
in a small office that was not big enough to

accommodate myself and the other three new auditors who started with me. We were given desks in another area of the floor that was filled with empty cubicles. There was not another soul on the floor and we had basically nothing to do. This was before the days of personal computers and cell phones, so I spent most of my time reading documentation and trying to learn whatever I could. I also spent time commiserating with the other three auditors about the mess we had gotten ourselves in.

The three new auditors and I had all transferred to the long-distance telephone company from a local exchange carrier (LEC). One came from Colorado, two from Illinois, and I came from Michigan. The core of the original auditing group in Chicago came from an equipment manufacturer, so we LEC auditors were pretty much considered outsiders. We didn't know the equipment company ways of doing things or their products and services. We were left alone to hang out in our little corner of the floor and get paid for doing nothing.

During this post-divestiture time, the way new companies and old companies did business with each other changed radically. For example, in the old days, when a call was made from Detroit to Minneapolis, the facilities used to complete the call belonged to the long-distance company, since the local companies on the originating end and terminating end were both subsidiaries of the long-

Robert Gray

distance company. There was a well-established
Division of Revenue process which allocated the
revenue from the call to the originating and
terminating companies. This process had been
done for years to ensure that all parties got their
fair share. However, after January 1, 1984, the local
companies were no longer subsidiaries. The long-
distance company owned only the long-distance
network and no longer had access to the actual
customers. Now the local companies were
suppliers who provided access to their local
networks so calls could be completed. The long-
distance company had to pay the local companies
for the use of their local network. So, on January 1,
1984, the long-distance company began receiving
bills for these access charges from all of the local
companies, including independent telephone
companies, from all over the country. The long-
distance company was being billed for millions of
dollars each month in order to complete its calls.
Bills came in on paper, tape, even in handwritten
form. Organizations were built to receive, pay, and
account for these bills. The goal was to pay them
before any late charges would accrue. But there
was no way to know if these bills were accurate.
Organizations were then formed to develop
processes and systems to verify the accuracy of the
bills. Typically, the bills were paid first, and then
verified. This is where the internal auditing
organization finally found me something to do.
Instead of doing internal audits, we became supplier

auditors, assessing the procedures and controls around access billing from the local companies.

I spent three years in this job, during which I traveled a great deal and led audit teams doing supplier audits. I was recruited to do this since I used to work for one of the suppliers, although I had very little knowledge of the areas being audited. It was obvious to me that the other lead auditors were much more well versed in the subject and I did my best just to hang on and not appear stupid. These supplier audits were often confrontational, which caused me to have a great deal of anxiety. I suffered from headaches during one of the engagements and had major stomach issues during another one.

In 1987, my father suddenly and shockingly passed away at the age of seventy-four. His death left me numb for quite a while since I had just seen him a week before. He had taken on a part-time job at a sandwich shop in Ann Arbor and, on Friday, February 20, he went to work and never came home. Just a few months later, a job in an organization which I was auditing within my company had an opening for a manager. I liked the district manager of the group (a very tall and attractive blond young woman), so I interviewed. We hit it off well and I was offered the job. I accepted it, probably more as a way to escape my auditing job than anything else, and felt lucky. Well, I found that I had jumped from the frying pan into the fire. I had eleven direct reports and they supervised a staff of about thirty clerical union workers. I also had three vacancies to fill and I was getting bombarded with calls and emails from people either wanting a job or recommending someone for a job. I had never been anyone's boss before and I was not trained in managing. I did the best I could based on my instincts as a human being. I found out that managing and being human do not go hand in hand. The stress I felt grew daily. I was no longer doing a job; rather, I was managing people who were doing a job. Sometimes I felt like a babysitter and I didn't understand why people were trying to take advantage of me.

After about a year, my boss realized that it was too much for me, so she hired another manager and divided the group in half. This new manager was experienced and was also a Navy man. He was known to most of the people in my group and had a reputation as a no-nonsense, do-it-my-way kind of a guy. He was well dressed, tall, and good-looking. Everything had to be just so with him, including how he tucked in his shirt. He was going to be tough and hold his people accountable. Most of the supervisors in the group wanted to work for me because they knew I was more easygoing. He was just what I needed. Around him, I felt inferior, afraid, and outmanned. My stress continued to grow to the point where I went to medical one day thinking I was having a heart attack. I felt like I did in business school. Things got so bad that a neighbor of mine invited me to lunch just to talk because he was afraid I was getting sick. Actually, he wanted to invite me to go on a New Warrior men's adventure weekend so I could work on my issues along with other men. (I did attend one of these weekends and participated in small groups for over a year. It was a positive experience and I made some changes in my life, but they were temporary.)

At one point, we were forced to downsize our organization and we had to let six people go. Based on the evaluations we had written, we identified the six. Three of them worked for me. The six employees filed an age-discrimination suit against us and we had to testify. During my testimony, I told the truth but it was obvious that they were trying to make me out as a poor manager. I took responsibility for writing honest appraisals and for not having done what a good manager should have done to help my people improve. I sobbed in front of everyone because I was so sorry this was happening, especially to one of the men whose wife was expecting. The legal staff told me I did a great job of falling on my sword, but I felt like the sword went right through my heart. I resented having to have gone through all of this.

Shortly after, our organization was being downsized and moved to Atlanta. I had no idea what I wanted to do but I knew that I was not going to be one of the lucky ones to survive the downsizing. I was not well connected in Chicago, so job possibilities would be limited. Lauren and I were blessed with triplets and we couldn't find an affordable house in the suburban area where we wanted to live. One day, I found out that my organization was going to be using national quality criteria to do a self-assessment. I had been working with these criteria for a while, so I contacted the man in New Jersey who was going to head the project. He knew very little about this, so I briefed him over the phone. He felt that I would be an asset to his project, so he hired me to work on the project, which eventually led to a full-time job in Atlanta. We were able to find a home we could afford and everything was looking up. However, my boss told me he thought I would never have finished the project without the help of someone in Atlanta who took over when I was having trouble meeting deadlines. Also, a vice president called me on the phone to ream me out because the results were lower than she expected. I was not used to being treated like this and I felt defeated and small.

By the time I got to Atlanta, the job had disappeared but they wanted me to take on another assignment which had direct reports. Oh no, not managing people again! Working in Atlanta was traumatic for me. I figured that the people who survived the downsizing were the best and the brightest and I was brought in as an afterthought. I perceived the atmosphere to be dog-eat-dog, take no prisoners, and I had trouble getting along or fitting in. There were several occasions when I cried after meetings when nobody was around. I never told Lauren or anyone else that I was having problems. I was too embarrassed. I managed to escape to a systems development organization as their quality manager. I didn't know very much about systems development but my role was to be part of the leadership team and to facilitate their meetings. I attempted to manage a small staff (again) who seemed to continue doing what they always did with little interference from me. My predecessor was an experienced manager and was very well connected throughout the organization. I came in as a veritable unknown who had big shoes to fill. One of my responsibilities was to help the leadership team implement process management. I was involved in reviewing other organizations in what became known as "guru reviews." I was one of the process-management gurus who would assess how well other groups were doing. My own organization gave process management a small amount of attention and I was unsuccessful at influencing them to pay any attention to anything other than budget issues. Although I was a failure locally, our headquarters organization respected me for my knowledge and gave me a job working for them. Now I was a member of the corporate quality office and was finally responsible for managing nobody. This led me to a position as a quality auditor, which is where I was when I accepted early retirement from my company. From there, I worked for several companies and was laid off or lost my job four times. I was fortunate to have good interviewing skills and a pretty good network so that I was never unemployed for very long.

Chapter Fourteen
Cybersex and Depression

In 1991, I was introduced to an online news service. I had heard about the internet and the ability to get news and email but I had not taken the plunge. A friend introduced me to it and I decided to set up an account. I didn't use it very often but it was fun to dial in and see what was going on in the world. A few years later, I was out of town on a business trip and was staying with a relative at his home in California. He introduced me to a popular online service. After browsing around a while, we entered a chat room. There was a conversation going on about a woman having trouble with a relationship. We watched the conversation and, every now and then, would join it—mostly for laughs. We took turns typing our comments but it was obvious that I was taking it more seriously than my cousin. He eventually left the room and I continued chatting. The woman on the other end was clearly interested in my opinion and she thanked me for chatting with her. For several days after that, I found myself going online as soon as I got back to their house from work.

Nobody else was home, so I dialed in and, using my cousin's account and identity, began to check out the various chat rooms. There were several categories of rooms with some intriguing names. I spent several minutes browsing around and getting involved in conversations just for fun. When I returned home, I quickly signed up for my own account. I didn't know it then, but this was the beginning of addictive behavior that would eventually lead to my severe emotional breakdown.

At the time, the online service company had a deal where the first five hours in a month were free. Anything over five hours would be charged to my credit card on a per-minute basis. I never paid much attention to this and I would easily pass the five-hour mark in a matter of days. I would make minimum payments on my credit card and, once it was maxed out, I would simply use a different one. The money didn't matter to me because making the minimum payments was easy and I was having fun. More importantly, I was feeling good. I was getting some kind of a rush from being online and I liked it.

My first online experiences were relatively innocent. I would explore the various chat rooms and follow some of the more interesting conversations. It was a no-holds-barred environment where people were just saying whatever they wanted to. Conversations were often flirtatious and sexual, and I noticed that some people were using private chat rooms to get away from the nonsense and to focus on each other. I was not interested in talking to men at all. Just women. I would look at user profiles and find out about people. If they seemed interesting, I would start up a conversation. I could do this for hours at a time and I found myself staying up later and later at night to satisfy myself. Some of the conversations led to cybersex and I was amazed at how easy it was to go there. There was no shyness in this cyberworld. I was a different person, with a great sense of humor, a gift of gab, and a desire to play. I was hooked. I was addicted to the high of fooling around in cyberspace. I never considered what I was doing was wrong or that I was being unfaithful. But, at the same time, I protected my identity and made sure that nobody could find me. I never knew who I was online with either. I only knew what was in their profile. And I believed it all to be true.

My desktop computer was located in the master bedroom of our home. Since I was a night owl, Lauren would usually go to sleep while I watched television at night, so it was not uncommon for me to be awake late at night. My online activity usually started at about 11:00 p.m. and, with the television tuned to *The Tonight Show*, I would sign on to the online service and spend some time in cyberland. At first, I would go online every now and then but it eventually became a nightly routine. Sometimes Lauren would wake up and ask me what I was doing and I would tell her that I was just chatting with friends. I would do my best to downplay it and hide my secret from her. We had a large master bedroom and, for no particular reason, we decided to rearrange the bedroom and moved the computer into the basement. I was hoping that this would limit my online time since it would not be so easy and convenient for me. This was not the case. As the lure of the chat rooms grew stronger, my willingness to take more risk did as well. I would leave the television on in the bedroom and go into the basement to get online with the hope that Lauren would not wake up and find me out of bed. On many nights, I would come back to bed in the middle of the night to catch a few hours of sleep before having to get up for work. I was careful to keep my identity hidden from my online friends. I was afraid that someone would stalk me or my secret would be uncovered if a woman knew who I was or how to find me. Over time, the need grew stronger and stronger. I started running into some of the same people night after night and relationships became more serious.

My first relationship was with Annie. We first met in a chat room and began conversing with each other. I could tell by her profile that she married and lived in another state. Our conversation began innocently enough. We were both online often and kept running into each other each night. She told me that she was a military wife and was in an unhappy marriage. She had been dealing with relationship issues as well as depression. I felt as if I was becoming invested in her well-being. She told me a great deal about her life, relationships, family, and unhappiness. It seemed like I was making her feel better about herself and her life. We didn't know each other's names and that was just how I wanted it. I was so afraid of being stalked by someone or having my secrets revealed, so I was very careful to be known only by my screen name. I knew what city and state she lived in based on her profile and, one day, she mentioned the store where she worked. I looked it up on a map and felt a sense of power, having information like this about her.

Our online conversations became flirtatious and eventually sexual. In the beginning, I felt like we were just having fun. We would type messages that were stimulating and suggestive and mutually masturbate. However, I got scared when Annie started telling me that she loved me and how unhappy she was in her marriage. She told me that she was on an antidepressant. I found out that she had two boys but she had also given up a son for adoption when she was a teenager. The father was a young man who was later killed in Vietnam. She always regretted giving up the baby and was trying to figure out how to find him. She often talked about meeting me and wanting to know my real name. I tried to slow things down on several occasions and even tried to stop logging into the online service. But I found myself drawn back to it over and over again. I started taking more risks by telling Annie my name. I gave her my office address so that she could send me cards in the mail. We probably chatted online every night for several months. She wanted to call me on the phone but I refused. I didn't want her to know too much about me or how to find me. I was afraid that she would just show up one day. However, that changed one night when I was traveling on business and realized that she could call my hotel and ask for my room. She called and we spoke for just a few minutes. When we hung up, both of us jumped back online. Each time I traveled provided another opportunity to give Annie a hotel telephone number and room number so that we could talk without me having to worry about being identified. After a few telephone calls, we took the next step to phone sex. But it was more than that. I felt like I was falling in love with her. I thought a great deal about the risks of this behavior and I often tried to stay away from being online. But the attraction was too great. I was addicted.

When I took on a new job reporting to New Jersey, there was no need for me to have an office in a company facility in Georgia. I moved my office to my basement and that provided me with the opportunity to accelerate into high gear. Now I had a company phone number that was not attached to my name so I could give Annie the phone number. I could make all the calls I wanted without Lauren discovering anything on our phone bill. So, now I had the computer and a phone in the privacy of my office in the basement. There was no way I would give Annie my home address, so she couldn't send me cards or letters anymore. I took care of that by renting a post office box at the local post office. Annie eventually stopped taking the antidepressant because she was feeling better about life. She left her husband, got a new job, and was much happier. She still wanted to meet me but I kept refusing. I did want to meet her and I was sad that we would never meet. But that was something that I couldn't allow to happen. During one of my business trips, we were only a few hours' drive from each other and it was so tempting. I kept looking on the side of the road to see if she might actually be waiting somewhere. Deep in my soul, I knew that meeting her would lead to something that I would always regret. But part of me wanted it to happen.

Our relationship continued for about two years. It wasn't always sexual. We had become friends. We talked about songs that we liked, such as "Kiss from a Rose" or "You Are Not Alone," whose lyrics meant something to us. I knew about her favorite constellation and her love of kites. I knew about her success in locating her son whom she had given up for adoption. She knew about my mother-in-law's passing and the Bat Mitzvah of my daughter. I knew she had met a man and started a relationship with him. I was happy for her and felt that I had contributed to her happiness.

But I felt a loss knowing that our relationship was ending. There was a song by Pearl Jam called "Black" that I would often hear and it would make me sad. The lyrics spoke about a man who lamented that a woman was going to have a great life with someone else, but not with him.

As our relationship started to wane, I got bored and I needed a replacement. I sought out more relationships. To me, it felt like a spider catching flies. I hung out in chat rooms looking for people to talk to and connect with. I also used the online profile information to spin my web. Searching for single or divorced females with a birthday was one of my favorite approaches. The search results would provide me with the information and I would check if they were online or not. If they were online, I would send them an instant message wishing them a happy birthday. Nothing more, just a simple happy birthday. Then I would sit back and wait. If the woman didn't respond, I would just let it go. If I did get a response, I would try to ensnare her in my web. Sometimes I would get a response like "Thanks" and then I would respond and see if a conversation would ensue. Sometimes I would get a response like "Do I know you?" or "Who are you?" to which I would say that I am just a friendly person who likes to send birthday greetings.

Ironically, the next relationship was with another military wife. Her name was Brenda. I used to see her in chat rooms quite often and she was definitely not shy in her use of language. I would hang out in rooms with her and I also got to know two of her friends, so we would often converse as a group. But there was something about Brenda that intrigued me. I learned that she had also been in the military and was now raising two daughters. I got the impression that she was emotionally abused, if not physically abused, by her husband. She would often send me poems and journal entries which described an unhappy life. I felt sorry for her and her situation and thought I could help somehow. She sent me a photograph of her in uniform and she was quite a bit younger and attractive. During one of our online conversations, she was telling me how unhappy she was and that she was crying. I could feel that this was the opportunity to pursue cybersex with her and see where she would go with it. I typed that I would wipe her tears away and kiss her cheek. She typed that she would kiss me back. Each time I pushed a little further, she followed my lead. We masturbated together online. I had caught another fly. Brenda and I also engaged in phone sex but our relationship did not reach the stage of wanting to meet. I discovered she was pretty wild online and I decided I had better steer clear of her. I stopped contacting her after a few months.

I had a few "one-night stands" and some partners who enjoyed being flirtatious whenever they were online. But the next relationship caused me, and the woman, a great deal of pain. Her name was Cathy; she was a divorced mother of two developmentally challenged young children. She flew into my web after I wished her a happy birthday. We had cybersex the first time we chatted with each other and it wasn't long before we exchanged telephone numbers. I still would never use my home or cell phone for fear of a call showing up on my bill and getting caught. I made calls to Cathy on my office phone or on the public phones in the area. For a dollar in quarters, I could talk for a few minutes. Sometimes I would go shopping at the local grocery store or stop for a tank of gasoline and I would sneak in a call just to say hello. If Cathy wanted to send me a card or a letter, I would have her mail it to the PO box which I rented. I was so afraid of getting discovered.

Things with Cathy got messy. She really wanted to get married again and she knew that would never happen with me. I knew that would never happen either but I didn't like the idea of her finding another man. I sent Atlanta Braves baseball caps to her kids. I talked to them on the phone. I even sent her money to help her pay her online service and phone bill. I felt strangely connected and extremely conflicted by this relationship. On the one hand, I knew that I would never meet her or give up my family for her. Yet, I was feeling very jealous and hurt by her talk of other men. She had arranged to spend a weekend with a man whom she had met online and I was enraged. I couldn't believe she would do such a thing and I was very concerned for her safety. It bothered me so much that I had trouble concentrating on my work and sleeping at night. She ended up having a horrible weekend with this man and she never planned to see him again. Then she told me that she was going to meet the brother of a good friend of hers. He was single and had suffered a brain injury and she wanted to see what he was like. She told me that she was going to spend some time with him and see if they hit it off. Once again, I got upset and angry. They began dating and got married soon after. Cathy thought it would be nice if our two families could meet someday and become friends. That was the last conversation I ever had with her. I was astonished to think how I would ever explain this friendship to Lauren and my children.

For several years, I was juggling relationships and trying to keep up with my life and my work all at the same time. I rarely went to bed before 2:00 a.m. but somehow I survived on adrenalin. I did my best to hide all of this from my wife and children. I often told myself that what I was doing was wrong and I knew that it had to stop. I tried to quit several times. I would stay off of the internet for a day or two and I would be happy that I was getting my life back. But the urges and the cravings were too seductive and I would find myself back in cyberspace again. I didn't realize then that I was addicted. After all, this wasn't a drug or alcohol. This was a behavior and I could just quit if I wanted to. Or so I thought.

One day in 1997, I encountered Darcy, a woman on the web whom I had met before. I remembered her because she lived in Ann Arbor, where I went to college. We started a conversation and hit it off immediately. She was divorced and had a son. Darcy was originally from St. Louis and we would talk about the 1968 World Series when my Tigers defeated her Cardinals. We spoke on the phone many times and became intimate. By this time, my need to be online had intensified. No longer did I require the privacy of my basement office. With a laptop, I was able to sit in the den and watch TV while the kids did their homework. As long as nobody could see my screen, I was free to flirt, chat, and plan our next encounter. The laptop also gave me the ability to work during the day on the laptop and have my personal desktop computer logged in to the internet at the same time. I could listen for that seductive "You've Got Mail" announcement or the sound of an instant message coming in. I now had the ability to be online almost all day. And if I ever had to go to the company office for a meeting, I would always try to find an empty conference room from which I could place a call to someone. Masturbating and having an orgasm with someone on the phone in a company building could have certainly gotten me fired but I was willing to take the risk. The risk made it more interesting and exciting.

Darcy would also call me when I was staying at out-of-town hotels. On one occasion, she found the address of one of the hotels and sent me a package. Unfortunately, the package did not arrive before I had to leave for home. I was so afraid that, when it did arrive, the hotel would send it to my home address and my secret life would be discovered. Luckily, I was back in New Jersey the following week, although in a different hotel. I called the hotel each day to try to track down the package. I was relieved when I found out that it had arrived and I went to pick it up.

Although I was afraid to actually meet any of these women, I realized that the geography could work out with Darcy. I believe that this was in the back of my mind when I reached out to her. Since I would be on campus for homecoming in the fall, it would be easy to arrange a meeting. We talked about it several times and I ran hot and cold. Sometimes I couldn't wait to meet her but other times, the idea scared the crap out of me. As the weekend approached, I began having major concerns about this meeting. I was concerned about infidelity, AIDS, and just how wrong I knew this was deep down inside. But I decided to go through with it. Lauren would be in Chicago for several days, so I packed my things and headed for Ann Arbor. When I left the house, I had a feeling of foreboding, as if I would be very different when I returned home. I felt that things would never be the same again but I decided to go for it and try not to worry. I was so very right. Things would never, ever be the same again.

I arrived in Ann Arbor on Friday. The football game would be played on Saturday afternoon. After getting settled in at my mom's house, I decided to take a drive toward Darcy's house. She told me she would be getting home from work in the early afternoon. I drove past her house and didn't see her red car. I knew all about her new car from previous conversations, so I knew what to look for. I left her neighborhood and headed away when I saw a red car going the opposite way. I thought it might be Darcy, so I turned around and went back to her house. Sure enough, it was her, so I rang the bell. She opened the door, gave me a big hug, and welcomed me in. She was so surprised to see me, since we had planned to meet the next night. We sat on the couch chatting for a while. I was very nervous about meeting her and about what we might do. What we might do ended up being oral sex.

When I left her house that afternoon, I felt awful. I couldn't believe what I had just done. I drove to a shopping mall to try to take my mind off of it. I returned to my mom's house, where we had dinner with my brother and his wife. It was a pleasant evening and I did my best to make it seem like nothing was bothering me. Later that night, I called Darcy and told her that I was not sure I should see her the following night. I was upset and I started feeling paranoid about contracting AIDS. She told me I had nothing to worry about because she had a steady male friend and everything would be okay. I didn't sleep much that night and was preoccupied during much of Saturday's homecoming football game with thoughts of fear and excitement. I decided to meet her again and we spent several hours together, once again engaging in oral sex. Darcy wanted more but I would not allow us to have sexual intercourse. Lauren and I were virgins when we got married and I just knew that sexual intercourse with this woman would be the ultimate sin. Once again, I left Darcy's house feeling awful. I had another night of tossing and turning, agonizing over recent events. I didn't expect to see Darcy again but my car battery was dead and I had to stay an extra day. On Sunday, I went to see her again with the intention of telling her that our relationship had to end. I told her how I couldn't sleep, how I couldn't live with myself for what I had just done, and how I could never forgive myself. I sobbed and wailed like a baby. Darcy must have thought I was out of my mind for reacting like this. But she said she understood and tried to tell me it would be all right. She led me upstairs and I was so terribly confused. We once again had oral sex and she told me as I was leaving that I should blame her for everything. How could I do that? I had crossed the line, betrayed my values and my family, and I felt like I had committed a terrible sin. I was ashamed of myself and completely guilt-ridden. I had been engaged in internet infidelity for a number of years and now this! Years of risking my family relationships, my career, my life!

The next day, I drove seven hundred miles to get home with the feelings of guilt and shame coming home with me. When I arrived home, my father-in-law and my kids were there to greet me. They were so happy to see me but I was in a fog. I went into the dining room, where I saw all of the mail that had arrived over the last several days. To me it looked like a tornado had come through and blown it all over the table. It looked like a great mess and I was angry that I would have to deal with it. There was one envelope that stood out. It was a different color and it was the size of a greeting card. I recognized the handwriting and saw that Lauren had mailed me a card from Chicago. I have absolutely no recollection of what the card said or what Lauren wrote. What I do remember is the feeling that a dagger had just been thrust through my heart and soul since I had betrayed the love of my life. In that instant, my sin had reached a new magnitude in my being and I had no idea how I would ever be able to live with it. For the next few days while Lauren was in Chicago, I couldn't sleep at all. I lay awake all night tossing, turning, and contemplating what I had done. I called Darcy and told her it was over and that I had to try to forget everything. I was frantic on the phone with her as I told her of my sleepless nights. Finally, after several nights of no sleep, I felt like I needed to confide in someone.

I went to see my father-in-law. I told him what I had done and how terrible I felt. I took a great risk and hoped that he would understand and be sympathetic. He took the news well and tried to tell me it would be okay. He suggested I call my rabbi, who told me that I needed to put it behind me and move on and take care of my family. I told him that I didn't think God would forgive me and he assured me that He already had. Forgiving myself would be the hard part. My father-in-law suggested we go out together, so we went to a local tearoom. Sitting with him and drinking hot tea felt relaxing. I started to feel better and he again told me it would be all right. Somehow, my twisted mind took that to mean that it would be okay to talk to Darcy. Suddenly, I felt a rush at the idea of speaking with her again. I called her and told her that everything would be okay. I told her that I talked to my father-in-law and I would be fine. She asked me if I was sure and I said yes but, at this point, I hadn't seen Lauren yet. When Lauren got home, I did my best to pretend that everything was fine. My biggest problem was my concern that I was now HIV positive. How would I be able to explain not wanting to make love? I worried about that every night at bedtime. I would try to stay up later so she would be fast asleep when I came to bed. My paranoia even carried over to being afraid to have my kids drink out of my glass. I started reading about AIDS and oral sex. I wondered if I had a cut in my mouth from playing my clarinet at the homecoming game that could have allowed me to get AIDS. I gave blood thinking that the Red

Cross would screen it for AIDS. I talked to people online about it, trying to use the expertise of total strangers. Some people told me that it could take up to six months for a test to come up positive, so I felt really screwed. Not only was I dealing with my sin and shame and trying to avoid my wife, now I was dealing the stress and uncertainty of disease. The last two months of 1997 were hell for me. My conversations with Darcy did continue for a little while. I urged her, almost demanded her, to get an AIDS test so that I would feel better about not contracting the disease but she refused, knowing that there was no need to do so. We actually discussed the possibility of meeting again in New Jersey when I would be there in early 1998. But she knew that we should terminate this relationship. The only time I heard from her again was after her regularly scheduled doctor visit. She emailed me to tell me she was HIV negative.

At the beginning of 1998, I struggled with giving up my internet activities cold turkey. I felt physically sick most of the time, so I went to a physician for a physical. At the time, I didn't have a regular doctor in Atlanta, so I actually flew to Detroit to see my previous physician. I stayed with my mom and pretended that I was on a business trip. Being back in Ann Arbor was difficult, being haunted by the memories of the recent past. I told the doctor what I had done, so he included an AIDS test as well. Everything checked out fine except I had H. pylori in my stomach and he wanted me to see a cardiologist because my EKG looked a bit unusual. I was convinced that I had contracted the virus from Darcy and that I was going to die of a heart attack. I was treated for the virus and there was nothing wrong with my heart. When I got the news, I was relieved, but for only an instant. The physical part of me was in good shape. The emotional part of me was sliding downward, faster and faster, out of control, and heading for disaster.

Chapter Fifteen
Treatment

In January 1998, I knew that I needed some kind of professional help. I couldn't go on living with this guilt and shame. First of all, I decided that I needed to move my office out of my basement. That space was full of bad memories and I thought I would feel better if I had an office around other people. Most of my organization was in New Jersey but one of my coworkers worked in a building in Midtown Atlanta, so I moved into a cubicle there. I contacted the company's Employee Assistance Plan (EAP) to get some help. I gave the consultant some information about my situation and he gave me a list of therapists in the area. I selected one of them, based on his name more than anything else, and made an appointment to see him. I told my wife that I was having some issues and felt like I needed to talk to someone. I tried to hide things from my wife but she was supportive of the idea. I called the therapist and made an appointment.

I had never seen a therapist before, so I didn't know what to expect. The waiting room was a pleasant little room with many choices for tea available. I sat down and waited to be called in. When it was my turn, I met the doctor and he

escorted me to his office. He asked me to tell him
about what brought me to see him and I unloaded
the whole story of woe and how I was devastated
by guilt and shame. His reaction was something I
will never forget. He said, "What a beautiful
story." What a beautiful story? Was he kidding
me? I had committed a terrible sin and was trying
to get over it and he thinks that my relationship
with this woman made for a beautiful story. I don't
know why I didn't immediately seek out a
different therapist but I stuck with this one for
about a month. I saw him once a week and I came
to the conclusion that I had to tell Lauren
everything. I remembered my rabbi telling me that
I needed to keep this to myself, live with it, get over
it, and forgive myself. My therapist agreed that
telling Lauren would be a mistake. There was no
need to drag her down with this. Sometimes the
truth is better left untold if it means hurting
someone unnecessarily. I should just man up.
People have affairs and keep it to themselves and
move on. Why can't I live with this? Why can't I
put it behind me? What would happen if I did tell
her everything? Our relationship could be
damaged forever. It could lead to divorce and the
breakup of my family. She could just kick me out
on my ass and I would be left to fend for myself.
Was there an upside to telling her? Nobody saw
one except me. And even my upside was a selfish
one. I figured that by telling her I would release all
of this guilt and shame and we could rebuild our

relationship, at least if she forgave me. If she didn't forgive me, well, I never believed that would happen. I hoped that she would somehow understand, I would be healed of my pain, and we would move on. I convinced the therapist that this was the best course of action and he agreed as long as the conversation happened in his office so he could be a mediator. I called Lauren with a sense of relief and told her to meet me that afternoon at the doctor's office. She agreed and asked if I had an epiphany. That was the first time I ever heard of that word. I would say that it had nothing to do with inspiration, rather it was desperation. I was out of options and I was willing to risk everything in the hope that the truth would free me from the pain.

I had several hours to kill until the appointment with my wife and the therapist. I spent the entire time driving with no particular place to go. I drove for miles and miles just to keep myself occupied. Driving was always something that I loved doing and I found it relaxing. As the time for our appointment grew near, I started heading toward the office. When I got there, Lauren and I sat in the waiting room and chatted. We were called back to the therapist's office and he told Lauren that I had something to tell her. I proceeded to tell her about my online relationships, the money I spent on the internet, and the meeting with the woman during my homecoming trip. I made it clear that we did not have sexual intercourse but we did engage in oral sex. I was extremely emotional and broke down crying while holding on to her. I don't remember everything that she said but I recall she said she needed to get tested for HIV. She was obviously angry and hurt but the fact that I did not have intercourse was at least something in my favor. After a while, I stopped crying and we decided to go home, where we would have to pretend in front of our four children that everything was okay with Mommy and Daddy. Many of the details of this appointment are no longer in my memory but there is one thing, one feeling that I absolutely remember. The truth did not set me free. I was not healed. Although it looked like Lauren might be able to forgive me at some point and there was hope that our family would survive, I still felt like a sinner. I still felt sick. There was a long, dark road ahead of me. This was not the end. This was only the beginning of the worst six months I could ever imagine.

I continued seeing this therapist for about two more months. Some of my appointments were joint sessions with Lauren. I have very little recollection about these sessions but I do remember trying positive self-talk. The idea behind positive self-talk is to catch yourself when you are thinking something negative and then to categorize it. Once you have determined what type of thought it is, you can then counter it with a more realistic, more positive thought. For example, I might think that I always make bad choices. The use of the word "always" means that this is a generalization and can't possibly be accurate. Of course, I make bad choices at times, but not always. So, I can counter that negative thought with something like "I have made some bad choices in the past but I am working hard to make better choices now." This is a more accurate and truthful statement of reality and it acknowledges that I am improving. The doctor gave me a worksheet to fill out to log my negative thoughts and how to counteract them. I made about twenty-five copies of this worksheet and began to fill them out. My statistical mind was thinking about histograms of the types of thoughts that came to my mind so I could analyze them and detect patterns. I took these worksheets to work and filled them out religiously. But eventually, I felt like this was not helping me at all, as I continued to feel bad. I stopped using the worksheets and my last entry was "I don't think I am doing this right." Sounds typical to blame myself for failing.

As far as work was concerned, I did my best to stay focused and keep doing my job. Moving my office to the Midtown location was a start since it got me out of the house and around people. I had a great deal of trouble concentrating and I would often leave work early. I decided to let my organization know about my problems and I sent out an email to everyone telling them that they may notice something different about me. I traveled to New Jersey in January for a team meeting (the trip when Darcy had talked about meeting again) and I felt so sick and out of place that it was most likely obvious that something was wrong. In my email, I said that I had been diagnosed with depression and I hoped that everyone would understand if my behavior had changed. I said that I had gone to EAP and was now under a doctor's care. I asked them to support me as best they could and to just be patient with me as I worked through this. I received a great deal of encouragement from my team and one person told me that she was suffering with depression and eating disorders, so she totally understood. She told me how brave I was to come out in the open and admit my illness to everyone. The responses I received made me feel better. At least everyone knew that something was going on with me and I didn't have to hide it. As the days passed, my condition worsened and my thoughts continued to plague me. I developed panic attacks, which caused me to pace back and forth. I was unable to sit still and I couldn't handle crowded places. Walking into a mall or a department store made me feel as if all of the people and displays were coming at me and I felt like running away to escape. I felt like I needed immediate help but didn't know where to get it. I would try to call my therapist and would hang up when I heard a voice mail greeting. I would try to call my rabbi and was dismayed to find out that he was unavailable. I would take the elevator to the EAP floor and pace back and forth wondering if I should go in or not. When I did go in, there was nothing they could do for me since they were not therapists. I didn't know where to turn and I got more frustrated, overwhelmed, and stricken with panic.

In my role at work, I was scheduled to accompany an independent auditor to Chicago, Columbus, and New Jersey. I made the arrangements for flights and hotels but I had no idea how I would survive this trip. By this time, I had so much trouble sleeping that I would listen to CDs of relaxing sounds to help me fall asleep. Though it helped a little, I was still getting very little sleep, which made me feel even more distraught. My stomach was such a mess that I could barely eat and I spent a good amount time in the bathroom. I flew to Chicago to meet the auditor. We had dinner together and checked in to our hotel. Dinner was a challenge since I had lost my appetite by this time. The next morning, we met in the lobby and I drove him to our first location. I managed to get through the day, which ended with a flight to Columbus. We got to our hotel late that evening and I tried to sleep with little success. Being in Columbus was especially horrible for me because Cathy lived near Columbus and the last thing I needed was a reminder of my sinful past. And if that wasn't enough, the occupant of one of the offices where we spent some time was a St. Louis Blues fan. Darcy was from St. Louis. The day in Ohio was uneventful and I got through it by drinking a lot of coffee to keep me going. Another flight that night to Newark was followed by a fairly long drive to Red Bank. That night was completely sleepless. My relaxation CDs did not help and my stomach was a mess. As the sun began to rise, I decided that there was no way I could make it through another day. I left a message for the auditor that he would be on his own, made arrangements for an earlier flight home, and got the hell out of there. By the time I got home, I was a physical and emotional wreck. I decided that I needed medication to get better. I was given the name of a psychiatrist and, after one appointment, he prescribed an anti-depressant. I don't remember which one it was but I wanted it to make me better fast. I had no patience for this illness and I hated the fact that I would have to wait a couple of weeks for it to start to take effect. The psychiatrist had no interest in my story and how I ended up in this condition. His job was to prescribe medication based on my symptoms. So, I took the medication but I never felt like it affected my condition at all. We tried other medications but nothing helped. Talk therapy wasn't helping, positive self-talk was pointless, and medication was useless. Was there any hope for me?

My physical exhaustion and emotional stress became paralyzing. I would go to work for as long as I could stand it and then get in my car, go home, and climb into bed. Eventually, I saw no point in getting up to go to work, so I just stayed in bed. I wasn't really sick and I told my wife I just didn't feel like going. After four consecutive days of staying home in bed, I got a call from the administrative assistant in New Jersey asking me if everything was okay since no one had heard from me. I told her that I was unable to go to work. She explained that a fifth day of consecutive absence constituted a disability situation. I told her that I didn't really care, so she told me to expect some paperwork in the mail. I would need to sign and return the forms so that I could go on short-term disability. This was of no concern to me at all since I couldn't even drag myself out of bed. I remained in bed doing nothing but watching ESPN on television for a few weeks. I would go downstairs for dinner on some days but I did little else. I stopped paying bills, taking out the garbage, bringing in the mail, and most other basic and mundane activities. I wanted no part of my family or any social activities. I just wanted to stay in bed and be left alone. All I could do was think about what I had done, where I was now, and how hopeless I was to ever regain my sanity and return to my old life.

After several weeks in bed, doing nothing but contemplating my condition, my exhausted mind reached a new conclusion. There was no hope for me, so maybe it was time to end it all. The emotional pain was becoming unbearable. The lack of sleep left me drained. The desperate feeling of helplessness and hopelessness fueled by guilt and shame led me to the conclusion that there was only one way out. I had no plan for how to take my own life and I certainly didn't want to die. But I didn't want to live like this anymore.

The thoughts of suicide were terrifying. I had always been afraid of death and tried to avoid the subject. Now I was actually pondering death as a viable option for me. I couldn't get the thoughts to stop and I was all alone and scared. I got dressed and drove to my father-in-law's house for help. I told him that I was contemplating suicide and couldn't get the thoughts out of my head. He made me call my therapist, who told me to get myself to a mental health facility immediately. He would call them to let them know I was on the way to be admitted. My main problem at this point was that I had no idea where the hospital was. I found the address and my father-in-law and I tried to figure out how to get there using a pre-GPS tool called a road atlas. We got in the car and tried to figure out how to get to the hospital. It was actually somewhat comical when you consider a suicidal person driving a car with a copilot who was unfamiliar with the area. We finally found the hospital where I was checked in and admitted. I don't even think I called my wife to let her know what was going on. At that point, all I could think about was needing help. While in the hospital, I was assigned to a different therapist who came to see me. My shoelaces and belt were taken away from me and I slept in the main area of the floor on suicide watch. I was given medication and participated in some of the activities. My family came to visit me and I played ping-pong with my kids. I don't remember much about the details of my hospitalization but I know that I was released to attend the Bat Mitzvah of a family friend, on the condition that I would return to the hospital later that day. I also remember participating in an activity where the patients built birdhouses from a kit. The combination of my ineptitude at building things and my nervous and shaking hands made this problematic. I wondered why they would allow a person like me to handle tools with which I could easily harm myself. It was determined that I was no longer suicidal and I signed a document to that effect. I was released and returned home, no longer suicidal but far from okay.

I somehow managed to make it through a birthday dinner at a local restaurant with my family. But Passover was another story altogether. We were invited to the home of some very good friends. I really didn't feel up to going but I gave it a shot. When we arrived, I became restless and began pacing. It felt quite uncomfortable to be around people. I just wanted to hide. The host of the Passover Seder asked me a question about the order for candle lighting because it was the Sabbath. All I could think of was that I couldn't care less about something so trivial and why was he bothering me with this nonsense. Under other

circumstances, we would have discussed it and
determined the appropriate way of handling the
Sabbath and the holiday. But on this night, the
whole thing meant absolutely nothing to me.
When it was time to begin the Seder, I took a seat
at the table, briefly. I was fidgeting in my chair and
feeling like I was going to jump out of my skin. The
panic was beginning and there was no way that I
was going to be able to get through this. I told my
wife that I had to go home. She understood and
drove me home. I took some medication and tried
to relax. She returned to the Seder. While I was
alone lying on my bed, the panic attack subsided
but my thoughts were racing. I felt like all I wanted
to do was throw myself over the bannister so that
I would land on the floor below. Probably not high
enough to kill myself, though. I called my wife and
told her she had to come home and stay with me. I
couldn't stand being alone. She left the Seder and
came home to stay with me and to calm me down
as I laid in a fetal position and trembled with
anxiety.

Weeks went by and my situation worsened by
the day. I became more and more reclusive and less
interested in the world around me. My bed was my
comfort zone and I stayed there as much as
possible. I went to my therapist for appointments
and sometimes my wife would join me. I was
making no progress and I finally decided to stay in
bed and skip the appointments. Sometimes, my
wife would call me on the phone to make sure I

was going to go only to find that I had no intention of meeting her there. It was pointless and I had pretty much given up. The longer I stayed in bed, the more I would ruminate on my predicament. Some people who suffer from depression are prone to hyperactivity within the brain and I was one of those. I just couldn't relax or turn off my thoughts, which often led me to some irrational conclusions. For example, I convinced myself that I was the devil using the number 666. My thinking involved some imaginative connections. I knew that three sixes was the number of the devil from the movie *The Omen*. The sum of three sixes is eighteen. In Hebrew, the letters *chet* and *yud* spell the word *chai* (life) and have the combined numerical value of eighteen, and I wore (and still wear) a *chai* necklace. So, it all made sense that I was the devil, especially when I incorporated the fact that my boyhood Detroit Tigers baseball hero, Al Kaline, wore the number six. Not only was I filled with guilt, shame, and suffering from depression, I was also an evil being who deserved to be punished by God.

In May, my daughter Aline finished the eighth grade, her final year in middle school, with an end-of-year celebration for the graduates. Somehow I dragged myself out of bed, got cleaned up and dressed, and went to the party. I milled around, trying to stay away from people, and managed to get through it. Interestingly enough, a photograph was taken of Aline and me and we both look so happy. Each of us still has the photo in our respective homes and, although it was taken at one of the worst times of my life, we look so happy. I'm sure I was anxious to get back in bed but, at least for a brief time, I was strong. By July, things had changed for the worse. My triplets, Hilary, Michael, and Eric, celebrated their ninth birthdays at Turner Field, where they took in a Braves game. I couldn't stand the idea of being around so many people and being away from my safe bed at home for that long. I chose to stay home. Some friends went along to help chaperone in my absence.

Thoughts of suicide persisted. I tried to ignore them or make them go away but to no avail. I used whatever logic I could muster to analyze my situation. I felt like I was standing at the edge of a bottomless pit. Moving in any direction away from the abyss led nowhere but back to the abyss. There was no way to escape the pain other than to jump into the abyss. There was no way to be forgiven for my sins other than to jump into the abyss. There was no way to erase the shame other than to jump into the abyss. Life had become too painful to endure. I thought nothing of the impact on Lauren and the kids. The only thing that mattered to me was to stop my suffering. The abyss offered the end of my pain. My life in exchange for peace seemed fair. Of course, the fear of eternal damnation in hell was an issue. Day after day, I struggled with these thoughts of life and death. One morning, I felt so desperate that I grabbed the keys to the car, went into the garage, climbed into the front seat, started the car, and waited. As I sat inhaling the deadly fumes, I began to think of the possible outcomes of my actions. If my suicide attempt was successful, I would be free of my suffering but I would be dead. If the attempt failed, and I was found unconscious, I would likely be locked up in a hospital for a long time. Neither outcome seemed acceptable, so I decided to shut off the engine and return to my bed. All in all, it was a pretty lame attempt at committing suicide. For that, I will be forever grateful.

By this time, my therapist determined that other treatments might be necessary for my recovery. Talk therapy and medications were having no positive effect. It was recommended that I see a therapist whose treatments included electro-convulsive therapy (ECT). I don't remember how many times I saw this therapist but I know that Lauren and I went together at least once. I also remember my reaction to the idea of having ECT. All I knew about ECT was that it was also called shock treatments and the visions of *One Flew Over the Cuckoo's Nest* came to mind. Brain-frying, lobotomy, and becoming an invalid didn't sound like anything I was willing to undergo. Lauren and I argued about it and she basically said that she could force me to have the treatments. She was willing to try anything to get me back. I was not so sure since I was the one who had to face the risk of having electricity passed through my brain.

Eventually, a date was selected for me to undergo the first treatment. I'm sure it was all explained to me and that the doctor did the best he could to allay my fears but I have no memory of any of this. All I remember is that, the night before the treatment, I could not sleep at all. Lauren stayed up with me all night and we talked. Sometime very early in the morning, Lauren fell asleep and I decided to run away. I snatched the keys to the car, snuck out of the house, and ran away from home. I decided to drive to Michigan. I'm not sure exactly what I was going to accomplish but I knew that was my destination. Was I planning to see the woman whom I had met there? Perhaps I was going to see my mother or my brother. I really had no idea but the thought of driving seven hundred miles was comforting since I had always found driving to be relaxing. I was afraid that the police would find me, so I took many back roads until I reached Oak Ridge, Tennessee. At that point, I got on the interstate and continued my drive.

Back at home, my wife realized that I disappeared with the car, so she called the police. I was mentally unstable but I hadn't broken any laws, so there wasn't much they could do. I wasn't gone long enough to be a missing person and there was no need to put out an APB for someone who just decided to go for a drive. My wife found out that the bank could put a trace on my debit card so that she could be notified when it was used. I stopped for food and gasoline at Exit 111 off of I-75, the

Bellefontaine Street exit in Wapakoneta, Ohio. This was one of our favorite places to stop on our family trips to Michigan since it was the home of Neil Armstrong, the first man on the moon, and almost every fast-food restaurant in existence. When Lauren was notified of my whereabouts, I'm sure she knew where I was going. When I arrived in Ann Arbor, I was still unsure about what I was going to do. I drove to Darcy's house but I didn't stop. There was a strange car in the driveway, so perhaps she had moved. I drove to my mother's house but I didn't stop there either. I drove aimlessly for quite a while until I decided I needed a place to stay. I tried several hotels in Ann Arbor only to find out that this was the weekend of the Ann Arbor Art Fair and there wasn't a room to be had. I parked my car in a shopping mall parking lot and tried to sleep. Falling asleep even in the comfort of my own bed was difficult enough, so trying to sleep in my minivan was next to impossible. In addition to being exhausted, I was hot, sweaty, uncomfortable, and helpless. After several minutes of restlessness, I decided to go home. I finally came to the conclusion that ECT was my last, best hope for recovery. I arrived home very late at night and Lauren decided to take me to the hospital to check in as soon as possible. She didn't want to give me the chance to escape again. The treatment would take place in the morning. I told Lauren that I wanted to take a shower, which greatly surprised her since I had not been interested in any form of

Robert Gray

self-care or hygiene for quite a long time. She asked me why and I told her that I felt grungy and needed a shower. Perhaps this was the first sign that I was really ready to get well.

According to Mental Health America (www.mhanational.org/ect):

> Electroconvulsive therapy (ECT) is a procedure in which a brief application of electric stimulus is used to produce a generalized seizure. It is not known how or why ECT works or what the electrically stimulated seizure does to the brain. In the US during the 1940s and 50s, the treatment was administered mostly to people with severe mental illnesses. During the last few decades, researchers have been attempting to identify the effectiveness of ECT, to learn how and why it works, to understand its risks and adverse side effects, and to determine the best treatment technique. Today, ECT is administered to an estimated 100,000 people a year, primarily in general hospital psychiatric units and in psychiatric hospitals. It is generally used in treating patients with severe depression, acute mania, and certain schizophrenic syndromes. ECT is also used with some suicidal patients, who cannot wait for antidepressant medication to take effect.
>
> ECT treatment is generally administered in the morning, before breakfast. Prior to the

actual treatment, the patient is given general anesthesia and a muscle relaxant. Electrodes are then attached to the patient's scalp and an electric current is applied which causes a brief convulsion. Minutes later, the patient awakens confused and without memory of events surrounding the treatment. This treatment is usually repeated three times a week for approximately one month. The number of treatments varies from six to twelve. It is often recommended that the patient maintain a regimen of medication, after the ECT treatments, to reduce the chance of relapse. . . .

After sixty years of use, ECT is still the most controversial psychiatric treatment. Much of the controversy surrounding ECT revolves around its effectiveness vs. the side effects, the objectivity of ECT experts, and the recent increase in ECT as a quick and easy solution, instead of long-term psychotherapy or hospitalization.

Because of the concern about permanent memory loss and confusion related to ECT treatment, some researchers recommend that the treatment only be used as a last resort. It is also unclear whether ECT is effective. In some cases, the numbers are extremely favorable, citing 80 percent improvement in severely depressed patients after ECT. However, other studies indicate that the relapse is high, even for patients who take medication after ECT. Some researchers insist that no study proves that ECT is effective for more than four weeks.

After my shower, Lauren and I drove to the hospital, where I was admitted. I remember very little about my experiences at the hospital. I assume this is due to the loss of short-term memory, which is often associated with ECT. However, what I do remember after my first treatment would qualify as miraculous. My room at the hospital was in a locked area. The ECT was administered in a separate area across the hall. It was performed in a relaxed setting and I wore my regular clothing during the procedure. I was given medication to relax me and then I was anesthetized. Upon waking up from the procedure, I found myself in a recovery room with several beds. There was a television set tuned to one of the local stations. I felt no discomfort or pain at all. As a matter of fact, I felt quite good. The room was brightly lit by the sunlight coming in through the windows and I felt a feeling that I can only describe as upbeat. I wasn't exactly sure where I was or what had happened to me but I was aware that what I was feeling was different. It was as if I had been stuck in a fog for a very long time and, all of a sudden, the fog was lifted from me. I could no longer touch the darkness which had plagued me. Once I had woken up completely, I was taken back to my room, where I continued to rest for a while. Later in the day, I phoned home to speak to my wife. I asked her if she would bring my electric shaver when she came to visit. She asked why and I told her that I looked terrible and needed to shave. She was surprised by my request, since my appearance and hygiene had not been a priority for quite some time. This was another sign that I was on the road to recovery.

I had about five more ECT treatments over the next couple of weeks but, because I was making such good progress, many of them were done on an outpatient basis. After some of the procedures, Lauren and I would go to a local restaurant for breakfast and then we would return home. My doctor prescribed an antidepressant and, in a few weeks, I was cleared to return to work. My company's EAP staff suggested that I start out slowly for an hour or so at first to see how I tolerated everything. I was feeling like that was unnecessary but I took their advice nevertheless. My return to work was uneventful and I was soon able to return to my regular work schedule. To me, it seemed as if nothing had happened to me. I was aware that I had been ill and that I had stopped going to work. But some of my memory of the events leading up to my hospitalizations and ECT were gone. One day in the fall, my family and I were visiting my mother in Ann Arbor. While we were there, I came across a slip of paper with a strange phone number in my wallet. I asked

Lauren if she knew what it was and she told me that the number belonged to a woman I had met and it was in my wallet just in case I ever needed it. I had no idea what she was talking about, so she explained it to me. I was shocked and stunned to learn of what I had done and I threw the paper away. Since then, many of the memories about that period in my life have returned. I have often wished that I didn't regain some of the memories. In the long run, however, they are a part of who I was, what I had lived through, and they formed the basis of my recovery.

Chapter Sixteen
Addiction

Throughout my entire illness and recovery, all of my treatment and therapy was focused on my mental illness. My diagnosis was severe depression and once I was on my way to recovery, my life basically picked up where it had left off. I returned to work and to my responsibilities as a husband and father. I continued with my career and even returned to school to earn a second master's degree, with a perfect 4.0. I completely stopped using online chat tools and was never again involved in chat rooms, cybersex, phone sex, or any other earlier behaviors. I am an avid user of social media, but I don't utilize it in any "bad" ways. I basically returned to normal, whatever that means. However, I was never treated for my sexual behaviors. I just quit and felt that it was all behind me.

In 2015, I became a Certified Peer Specialist for the Georgia Mental Health Consumer Network. One of the activities used at the center where I worked is called Double Trouble Recovery (DTR). It is designed to support people in recovery from a mental health challenge as well as any addiction issues. Peers who have a dual diagnosis attend these activities and utilize a twelve-step process to

Robert Gray

aid in their recovery. One day, I asked if I could sit in since I was on staff and had no familiarity with these meetings or the twelve-step process. During this first meeting, I observed and listened to the peers talk about their addictions to drugs or alcohol. I soon discovered that some of the things I heard resonated with me and their addiction experiences were very similar to my cybersex issues. For the first time, I realized that I was an addict and my drug of choice was cybersex. I began studying the twelve-step process and learned that I had a lot of work to do. I had never truly forgiven myself for my cybersex behaviors and had never realized how helpless I was. In order to truly overcome my addiction, I needed to work the steps and attend these meetings. Even though I had not engaged in cybersex or phone sex for eighteen years, I still had work to do to accept and understand that I was indeed an addict and needed to keep working on my recovery.

The twelve-step process used in the DTR meetings is documented in *The Twelve Steps and Dual Disorders: A Framework of Recovery for Those of Us with Addiction & an Emotional or Psychiatric Illness* (Hazelden Publishing; April 29, 1994). There is also a workbook accompanying the text. The twelve steps for double trouble in recovery are as follows:

Step One: We admitted we were powerless over our dual illness of chemical dependency and emotional or psychiatric illness—that our lives had become unmanageable. A core principle behind the First Step is recognizing that we have two chronic disorders—chemical dependency and an emotional or psychiatric illness. These two no-fault illnesses are creating big problems in our lives. That every way we have tried to cope with these problems has not worked. We simply cannot do it alone. Help is required.

Step Two: We came to believe that a Higher Power of our understanding could restore us to sanity. A core principle behind the Second Step is coming to believe that there is a source of wisdom, courage, and strength, greater than ourselves, that we can tap into that will help us to hope, cope, and heal.

Step Three: We made a decision to turn our will and our lives over to the care of our Higher Power, to help us to rebuild our lives in a positive and caring way. A core principle behind the Third Step is making a commitment. We decide to let go of our old, ineffective ways and begin to look to our Higher Power for the guidance and resources we need for dual recovery.

Step Four: We made a searching and fearless personal inventory of ourselves. A core principle behind the Fourth Step is to identify our assets and liabilities for recovery. Things that will help us in dual recovery and the things that will harm our dual recovery. It's an opportunity to start identifying and healing the pain from the past and to stop the progression of our illnesses.

Step Five: We admitted to our Higher Power, to ourselves, and to another human being the exact nature of our liabilities and our assets. A core principle behind the Fifth Step is that in sharing our list of assets and liabilities, we learn more about ourselves, see through our blind spots, find out what is true, where we are misguided, and what areas we need to work on.

Step Six: We were entirely ready to have our Higher Power remove all our liabilities. A core principle behind the Sixth Step is that we review what we have done in the first five steps and decide if we're ready for the new life offered in dual recovery. Being ready involves a clear decision, a commitment. We must be willing to let go of our old ideas to make way for new ones.

Step Seven: We humbly asked our Higher Power to remove these liabilities and to help us to strengthen our assets for recovery. A core principle behind the Seventh Step is taking the actions required to move forward in our dual recovery. We ask for and follow the good advice we are given.

Step Eight: We made a list of all persons

we had harmed and were willing to make amends to them all. A core principle behind the Eighth Step is preparing ourselves to mend relationships and get ourselves prepared to do our part to repair any hurts we have caused others.

Step Nine: We made direct amends to such people wherever possible, except when to do so would injure them or others. A core principle behind the Ninth Step is cleaning up the wreckage of the past. We don't need any old baggage holding back our spiritual growth and personal dual recovery.

Step Ten: We continued to take personal inventory and when wrong promptly admitted it, while continuing to recognize our progress in dual recovery. A core principle behind the Tenth Step is learning to examine our thoughts, feelings, and actions on a daily basis. So that we can fix things or set them right as soon as possible. This frees us to focus on our dual recovery, live in harmony, and continue to grow on a day-by-day practical level.

Step Eleven: We sought through prayer and meditation to improve our conscious contact with our Higher Power, praying only for knowledge of our Higher Power's will for us and the power to carry that out. A core principle behind the Eleventh Step is to continue to live in the solution by making sure our thoughts, feelings, attitudes, and values are in line with what our higher or helping power wants for us.

Step Twelve: Having had a spiritual awakening as a result of these Steps, we tried to carry this message to others who experience dual disorders and to practice these principles in all our affairs. A core principle behind the Twelfth Step is that once we've experienced the benefits of working the Steps, we will want to continue to strengthen our own dual recovery by helping others and doing service work. We continue to live by and practice the principles found in the Steps every day.

Chapter Seventeen
Cybersex Addiction

After working on my addiction issues, I became interested in the specific area of cybersex addiction. Much of the information on the subject began to appear in the mid to late 1990s, precisely when I began my descent into the world of the internet. The first internet addiction study was launched in 1994 by Dr. Kimberly S. Young, who eventually founded the Center for Online Addiction. Internet addiction was not recognized by many therapists at that time since it was such a new development. Perhaps that explains why I was never diagnosed or treated for addiction. Since then, with the explosion in technology, the increase in the spread of cybersex and pornography has skyrocketed. The ease of sharing messages, photos, locations, and videos has put cybersex into the hands of practically everyone with a cell phone. Our society has created new words, such as "sexting," to account for some of this behavior.

In a 2010 article entitled "The Seven 'As' Contributing to Internet-Related Intimacy Problems: A Literature Review," Katherine M. Hertlein and Armeda Stevenson identify seven key contributing factors for the rise of cybersex and infidelity:

1. Anonymity: The ability to be anonymous, or to use a fictional personality, removes a great deal of the risk. During my early experiences with cybersex, I took great measures to protect my identity as well as my location. I was fearful of being stalked or found. I didn't want to run the risk of getting caught in the act. Everything had to be a secret. Only my screen name was known, and my profile contained no iden-tifying information. Over time, I allowed some information to be known as I became more willing to take more risks to fuel my addiction.

2. Accessibility: Anyone with a cell phone and an internet connection can access practically anything. Parental controls can only do so much to keep children away. Firewalls and prohibiting websites can help to some degree. However, even a student doing research on pornography for a school paper will likely see images and videos. There is no way to police the entire internet. It is there for the viewing.

3. Affordability: In the 1990s, there were offers for free internet service for the first five hours every month. I would normally rack up monthly bills in the neighborhood of $200 to satisfy my needs. Making cell phone calls was not inexpensive either. But today, the internet and cell phones are generally billed as flat-rate

services. There is no need to worry about how long you are connected. It's a great deal for someone who can't stay disconnected.

4. Approximation: Cyber experiences can be almost as good as the real thing. Perhaps as good as or even better than. In the fantasy world, a person can create personas, situations, live out fantasies, and get the same rush of excitement. It's the next best thing to being there.

5. Acceptability: So many people are, or have used, the internet for sexual purposes. Whether for casual browsing, flirting, or other forms of pleasure, it has almost become an acceptable part of life. In addition, many people don't view cyber relationships as infidelity. After all, there is no real, physical intimacy going on. It's all just for fun. I used to tell myself that too. But I knew I was lying to myself.

6. Ambiguity: Many people don't view cyber relationships as infidelity. After all, there is no real, physical intimacy going on. It's all just for fun. I used to tell myself that too. Another issue is where does one draw the line between what is just for fun and what is not? Some people might consider viewing pornography as acceptable behavior while others might not. And what if the behavior begins to take over one's life and is no longer just an infrequent occurrence? When does cyber behavior move into the category of infidelity or illness?

7. Accommodation: This refers to the conflict a

person might have between their real self and their ideal self. A person may lead a relatively boring, average life but, on the internet, they can become someone else, perhaps someone they would rather be.

Chapter Eighteen
Recovery

After my ECT treatments were over, my doctor continued to see me on a regular basis and he prescribed an antidepressant. I kept all of my appointments and took my medication religiously. As far as I was concerned, I felt fine, but I didn't want to take any chances. My return to work was uneventful and I began working a regular schedule shortly after my return. My oldest daughter, Aline, was starting her freshman year in high school and was beginning her marching band career. Since I had been in the marching band at Michigan, I took a great interest in her band experience and I would often attend her rehearsals. This was a source of irritation for her since I had not cared at all about her for several months and now, all of a sudden, I was interested again. This is pretty much how things went. I had returned to life from the dark and dismal depths of depression and cybersex. ECT somehow rebooted my brain as if the doctor had found the Ctrl-Alt-Del buttons on my mental and emotional keyboard. The darkness which had enveloped me had somehow lifted, and I was now surrounded by light again.

My illness was something that I was not proud of, and I rarely spoke of it. Some of my closest relatives and friends were only aware that I had been ill and was hospitalized. I didn't provide any information at all about my situation or my illness. "I'm doing a lot better" or "I feel fine" was about all I was willing to share. The first time that I ever spoke publicly about my mental illness was about seven years after my ECT. I was teaching high school mathematics through a program where businesspeople were being hired and trained to be teachers. After being laid off from my job, I decided to try my hand at teaching. I had always loved mathematics and was able to relate well to kids, so it seemed a natural fit. During the summer, I took a class called The Exceptional Child. The class was focused on understanding the needs of students who had various conditions such as autism, Asperger syndrome, and various other physical and emotional conditions. One of the sessions dealt with depression, bipolar disorder, and other diagnoses. We often had guest speakers come in and talk to the class, so I asked the instructor if I could talk to the class about my depression. She agreed and I put a presentation together. Many people are fearful of public speaking, but that is not one of my issues. I love being in front of people and making presentations. So, I presented my story of depression and recovery and talked a lot about how it feels to be depressed. I answered many questions and the teachers told me that they enjoyed my talk. I left out many of the more personal details, but I found it easy to talk about my mental illness. A few years later, I discovered the National Alliance on Mental Illness (NAMI). NAMI is an organization that provides support and education for consumers (those who utilize mental health services) and for their family members.

I had never heard of NAMI or any other group involved in mental illness. I heard that they had an affiliate in my county, so I did some research and decided to get involved. I got up the nerve to call the president of the local affiliate, and we had a very nice conversation. She was excited about my enthusiasm and my interest in what I could do for NAMI. It just so happened that they were about to hold elections for their board of directors, and they needed a vice president. I told her I would be interested in running for the position and, at the next meeting, I was elected after running unopposed. Welcome to the world of volunteer organizations.

One of the first things I learned during my involvement was how little I knew about mental illness and the challenges that others and their families faced. I learned that, by recovering on my own, I had my own stigma about people with mental illness. I saw myself as being different from everyone else. Because I was never homeless, strung out on drugs, or incarcerated, and having a BA, MBA, and an MSQA, I felt that I was better than other people. I had a "white collar" mental illness. Just a few months after becoming involved

Robert Gray

with NAMI, I took a class to learn how to present my story in public speaking engagements. The program is called In Our Own Voice (IOOV) and it is designed to provide a structured approach to speaking about our own personal stories of illness, recovery, and hope. The presentations are comprised of five sections: Dark Days, Acceptance, Treatment, Coping Strategies, and Successes, Hopes, and Dreams. According to the NAMI website, "NAMI In Our Own Voice presentations change attitudes, assumptions, and stereotypes by describing the reality of living with mental illness. People with mental health conditions share their powerful personal stories in this free, 90-minute presentation." In a NAMI In Our Own Voice program, people with mental health challenges share their powerful personal stories. People who attend the presentation will hear what it is like to live with a mental health challenge. They will learn that everyone can hope for a better future and have a chance to ask questions. In the class, I met people with various mental health challenges. Some people didn't speak as well as others, some didn't write as well as others, and some people had jobs while others did not. People from different walks of life, different socioeconomic backgrounds, different faiths, but we all had one thing in common: recovery from a mental health challenge. As I learned more about each person and their story, I began to realize that I was no better or no worse than anyone else. I was not special. I was just ignorant about the many people who had struggled with a mental illness and had come out on the other side and were ready, willing, and able to talk about it. As the class progressed and we worked on writing and presenting our stories, there was a moment when I broke down and cried. The tears were not caused by remembering the pain of my mental illness. Rather, they were caused by a feeling of shame for having such a stigma about people with mental illness, including myself. Other than my hospitalizations, I had never been in a room with so many people with mental health challenges. Thinking about attending the class, I had some anxiety about meeting people. I didn't know what to expect. I felt like I was different. When I realized that I was the same, no better or worse, and I realized how everyone accepted me, I cried because I had a long way to go toward accepting myself.

Throughout my life, I had always considered myself to be a negative thinker. I generally held a pessimistic attitude and I would half-jokingly rationalize by saying that if I think negatively there is a negative result, then I get what I expect. If there is a positive result, then I get a pleasant surprise. There is no way for me to be disappointed. When I started hearing and reading about positive thinking and the Law of Attraction, I became intrigued. I spoke to several people who believed in quantum physics and learned about vibrations and flow. I was told that I had to ask the Universe for what I wanted and the Universe would make it happen. It seemed crazy to me but I was willing to learn more. I found a book called *The Secret*, which is also a movie. I began to read it, but it seemed too farfetched for me. I was unwilling to believe that healthy thoughts make you healthy, thoughts of abundance lead to abundance, and positive thinking brings positive things into your life. It was too much for me to accept, so I stopped reading the book.

I also heard about a movie called *What the Bleep? Down the Rabbit Hole*. This movie had some fascinating interviews and stories that talk about the link between quantum mechanics, neurobiology, human consciousness, and day-to-day reality. I suppose there was enough science in the movie to make it more believable to me. It opened up my imagination enough to give it some serious consideration. My training in quality assurance taught me to look for the root causes of problems, so I decided that I needed to understand the root causes of my negative thinking. Several years ago, I tried positive self-talk to combat my depression, but I was not in the right frame of mind for it to work. Perhaps now things would be different. I felt that I needed help to dig into my past and my beliefs about myself and the world, so I contacted a friend of mine in a professional capacity. My friend was a psychologist. I asked him to help me understand the way I think. During our sessions, we talked a lot about my upbringing, my Holocaust survivor parents, my older brother's shadow, and many other things from my childhood and formative years.

Growing up in a generally negative environment conditioned me to think negatively. That made sense to me, but I still needed help understanding how changing my thinking can help. My friend asked me to try a simple little test. One of my issues has to do with authority figures or people at high levels within an organization. I feel like they are unapproachable and wouldn't want to talk to me because they are better than me. The test was for me to go up to someone who is at a senior manager level and to say something nice to him. I should say something complimentary, but it had to be sincere. I couldn't just make something up that wasn't true. One day, I had a chance to say something to one of the senior VPs in my organization. I introduced myself to him. He knew of my organization but didn't know me personally. I told him that I thought his program to teach employees about the benefits of collaboration was a great idea and that I was happy to be involved in the training. I could see how valuable the classes were, and I congratulated him for implementing the program. He thanked me for saying that, we shook hands, and went our separate ways. I was feeling good about telling him that. A day or two later, we saw each other again. He said hello, shook my hand, and said he hoped I was having a good day. I felt good that he remembered me and that he greeted me pleasantly. When I told my psychologist about the experience, he showed me how positive thinking was at work. I approached the manager in a positive way, I said something positive to him, and I got a positive result. I felt good about having a positive experience.

It was a small test, but I started to get the message. This small discovery was a major turning point for me in my recovery. It opened my mind to many new ideas, and it led me to discoveries that continue to occur every day. I believe that this one small change has played a large part in making me a better husband and father. It has helped me to turn difficult situations into successes and to embark on a new career. If I hadn't changed my thinking, I would never have written this book.

Not long after I started seeing my friend the psychologist, I had the opportunity to see my wife's aunt. I remembered that she had done some reading about positive thinking and the Law of Attraction, so I talked about it with her. She told me about some of the books she had read and how she has been practicing using positive thinking in her life. I was fascinated by what she said and how strongly she believed in it. Ironically, or perhaps by design, the next time Lauren and I visited Michigan we stayed at her home. She was kind enough to give up her bedroom for us and, while I was getting ready for bed, I took a look at the books on the shelf. All of a sudden, I spotted a book and I felt like it almost jumped off the shelf into my hands. The book was called *The Key to Living the Law of Attraction* by Jack Canfield. I read the back cover of the book and checked out the contents. I was convinced that I had to read this book. In fact, I read a great deal of it before going to sleep and finished it the next day. It was a short book and an easy read, but it was a book that opened my eyes to new ways of thinking, and I would read it again several more times over the next few years. To quote Jack Canfield, "Simply put, the Law of Attraction states that you will attract into your life whatever you focus on. Whatever you give your energy and attention to will come back to you. So, if you stay focused on the good and positive things in your life, you will automatically attract more good and positive things into your life" (www.jackcanfield.com/blog/using-the-law-of-attraction). I decided to heed his advice and live my life focusing on good and positive things.

Chapter Nineteen
Me? A Runner?

One of the first things I chose to focus on was my physical health. I had been overweight most of my life and, although I had been walking quite a bit to train for the Susan G. Komen 3-Day, which I did twice, I was still overweight. My daughters each told me that they were concerned about me being overweight and they didn't want me to get sick. That was enough to motivate me to do something about it. I went on a weight-loss program and kept telling myself that I would succeed. I was able to lose eighty-four pounds and I felt very good about myself and what I could accomplish. At the time, I worked in Midtown Atlanta, across the street from the track at Georgia Tech. It would be easy for me to go to the track during lunch time and walk. I would slip on my sweats and a T-shirt and head over to the track. There I was, walking my laps for about twenty minutes, and watching the young athletes practice their field events and running on the track. They would nod at me and say hello, and I would joke with them that they should try their best to keep up with me. After several days of walking on the track, I began to wonder if I could run at all. As a boy, I absolutely hated running. I was very slow in short distances and had no stamina at longer distances. In junior high school, we had to do a six-hundred-yard run. I could never do it without walking. I felt like I had too much weight to carry and I just couldn't breathe. In college, I injured my right knee playing football in the mud. This injury led to MCL repair surgery, and my knee hurt every day after that. I wasn't able to extend or bend it fully, so running was something I never thought I could do. But when I was in my twenties, a friend of mine convinced me that I should try jogging. I still remember my first attempt to run around the block in my neighborhood. The total distance was 1.2 miles. I completed it but I walked about one mile and ran the other 0.2. I was huffing and puffing and every part of me was in pain. But I didn't give up. I went out every other day and kept trying. It wasn't long before I could jog the entire 1.2 miles, and then 2.4 miles became easy. The most I ever ran was about four miles. Then my daughter Aline was born and we moved to Illinois. I ran off and on after the move until I sprained my ankle while running at night. That marked the end of my running career for a long time. Several years later, we relocated to Georgia and I suffered an ACL tear in the same knee. More surgery, more physical therapy, more pain, and more fear that my knee would never be good. So, this thought about running at the Georgia Tech track may not have been the wisest thing I've ever thought of.

I decided to give it a try. My first attempt at

running one lap (one-fourth of a mile) was about as expected. I couldn't finish the lap, but at least my knee felt okay. There was some pain, but nothing out of the ordinary. In only a few days, I conquered the one-fourth of a mile barrier. The next day, I ran a little more. Each day, I would set out to extend the distance, even if only a few yards. Each time I succeeded, I felt better about myself and my abilities. I would run with my earphones and I discovered that the rhythm of the music helped me to pace myself. It didn't have to be inspirational or motivational. As long as I could match the speed of the music, it was all good. The most surprising thing was how much I enjoyed running. I actually looked forward to lacing up my shoes and heading out. The following spring, Lauren's school was sponsoring a fun run called the Husky Hustle 5K. I had never entered a race before and I didn't know how I would handle the distance, but I decided to enter. After all, it was a fun run for a good cause. It was a very nice, cool morning and I had a great run. I didn't run every step of the way, but that was not one of my goals. I just wanted to finish and have a good time. I got my first T-shirt as a runner and I wore it proudly. But this was only the beginning.

I continued running and decided to enter the Peachtree, the annual 10K event in Atlanta on the Fourth of July. Thousands of people enter this race every year. Many of the entrants are serious runners, but the majority are just in it for the fun.

Many people wear patriotic costumes, and it has become a big party event. It was very hot and humid that morning and I found the run to be very difficult, especially the famous uphill climb. But I finished and got another T-shirt. Running had become a habit and the more I did it, the better I felt about myself. Atlanta has a half-marathon in the fall, so I set my sights on that as my next goal. The biggest obstacle I faced was not the distance. Rather, it was running without music. The race rules stated that runners could not use earphones or other sources of music so they could hear course instructions and things going on around them. I had to find other things to keep my mind occupied and to pace myself. I also needed a plan to get ready for this race. I found a training schedule and read a book about marathon running. I followed the training schedule religiously. If the weather was unfavorable, I would run anyway. I would run in the morning, after work, or at night as my schedule allowed. The most important thing was that I ran when I didn't feel like running. Many people told me that the hardest step of any run is the step going outside. This was often the case when I had to drag myself out of bed early in the morning or when it was hot and humid. I maintained my discipline and my focus on my goal. As far as running without music, I discovered some interesting things that kept me going. Positive thinking helped a great deal to motivate me. Sometimes, I would sing songs to myself to maintain my rhythm. One of my favorite songs to sing was "Me and My Shadow." It had a nice, slow beat that matched my pace. And, it meant something special to me because I would see my shadow running on the pavement and I would figure that I must be running too. That would make me laugh at myself.

I also discovered that if I were to smile or think about things that made me happy or grateful, it would make my pain go away, steady my pace, and keep me going. I would think about how lucky I was to have a wonderful family and how fortunate I was to have the strength and ability to be running at my age. I would think about my depression and how far I had come from the days of suicidal thoughts and ECT. I had so match to be grateful for and thinking about those things helped me run longer distances. The day of the race came and I was ready. I had been using the Jeff Galloway approach of run sixty/walk thirty during training and I was comfortable with it. It was a great day for a run and I handled the distance well. As I made the final turn heading for the finish line, I spotted my son Michael on the sidewalk and he was cheering me on and running with me. All of a sudden, I felt the kick that runners often have when they need to go all out to finish a race. I was striding confidently, smiling, and feeling wonderful. As I reached the finish line, I pumped my fists in celebration of a great accomplishment. I didn't care one iota about my time or my

placement. I just wanted to finish and feel the joy
of doing something I never thought possible. I ran
another half-marathon, this time with Michael and
his wife-to-be Jessica (yes, I got them interested in
running too) and I started entertaining thoughts of
running a full marathon. I figured that if I trained
hard and stayed focused on my goal that I could
do it. I read more about marathon running and
training and began looking for races. I decided that
the Marine Corps Marathon would be the one for
me. It provided a pretty flat course and it was held
in late October, so the weather would probably be
pretty cool. With my daughter Hilary going to
school at George Washington and living in
Arlington, I would have a place to stay and have a
chance to see her. In February, when the website
opened for signing up for the marathon, I was
sitting in a coffee shop, eagerly awaiting the time
when I could enter the race. At the appointed hour,
I tried to complete the application for the race, only
to find that the website was not responding.
Apparently, there were so many people trying to
access the site that it couldn't handle the traffic. I
tried over and over again. Sometimes I was able to
get through, but I would eventually be timed out.
I checked into a social media site and found a page
for the marathon. To my dismay, many people
were posting that they were having the same
frustrating experiences as I was. People were
commenting that they couldn't get in or the site
would time out. After a couple of hours, the site

officially closed and no more entries would be accepted. I was feeling devastated that I would not be able to accomplish my goal of running the marathon. But then, I saw that people were posting about entering the race through a fundraising organization. Suddenly, there was a glimmer of hope. I went to the marathon site and was able to access a list of organizations that had spaces available. I landed on the Lung Cancer Alliance, which had a team called Team Lung Love. My wife was a lung cancer survivor, having had a third of her right lung removed. This was the perfect organization for me to run with. I would have to raise money for the Lung Cancer Alliance, but I was no stranger to that since I had raised money for breast cancer before. I went back to the website and found the link to sign up for Team Lung Love. To my delight, the transaction went through and I received an email confirmation. I still didn't really believe it, so I sent an email back to the Lung Cancer Alliance asking them to verify that I was actually going to be able to run the race. The response came back saying that I did have a spot and that I would be receiving a welcome package in the mail. I began to cry, knowing that I would have the opportunity to run the race. I had no doubts that I could do it, but I knew that I had a lot of work ahead of me.

I planned out a running schedule that would cover about four months of training. I would do two runs during the week and then a longer run on the weekend. The distances would build over time so that each week I would be increasing my total miles. I had some time to prepare before the actual schedule would begin. I decided to start running for a certain amount of time without worrying about distance or pace. I figured that I needed to build stamina more than anything. I started running thirty minutes each time and then, when I was comfortable with thirty minutes of running, I would add two minutes. It wasn't long before I was able to add two minutes to each run. I did a lot of these runs on a track, but I never got bored with running on the oval. I kept my mind focused on positive thoughts and gratitude. I sang my songs to myself to keep my pace steady. The hardest thing was to ignore the stopwatch. Looking at the time too often could discourage me. But there was one positive aspect to the time. Regardless of how many minutes I was to run, after I hit the halfway point, running would become easier, as if I knew I could make it from here. I used to love seeing the halfway point.

When I started the actual training program, I decided to run on sidewalks so I could get used to the harder surface since the race would be run on the streets of Arlington and DC. After several weeks of running, I noticed that the heels of my running shoes were wearing out. I thought this was unusual, so I went to a local running store for advice. They had me run on a treadmill and videoed my feet as I ran. Upon analyzing the video, they diagnosed that I was overstriding, which caused me to land on my heels rather than the balls of my feet. This also meant that I was landing with my legs straight so that the impact would likely take its toll on my knees. Since my right knee was an issue after having two operations, this was not going to be a good thing for me. I purchased a pair of zero-drop running shoes and enrolled myself in a class to learn Good Form Running (GFR). I learned how to use my arms and my legs properly and how to avoid overstriding. It took a while to get used to it, but I kept working on it. I was still doing a lot of walking during my longer runs, so I was hoping that this improved running style would help. My next weekend run was a thirteen miler. I decided to try as hard as I could to run as long as possible without walking. As usual, the first mile or so was difficult since I typically take a while to get comfortable and get into my rhythm. I concentrated on my running technique to use my large leg muscles for power and not my knees as pendulums. I tried to keep my arm swing straight so I didn't cause my hips to rotate. And I tried not to land on my heels. When I was using the GFR technique properly, running seemed to be easy. Everything worked together and I wasn't fighting to keep going. It was easy to tell when I would deviate from the GFR technique. I would feel like I was working too hard and I wasn't using my leg muscles for power. I would start breathing harder and feeling more tired. But I was able to recognize what I was doing and revert back to GFR. It was a very peaceful run and, when I got close to the end, I realized that I hadn't walked a single step. I finished the run and felt jubilation for my accomplishment.

Of course, I had several runs during the course of my training that left me thinking that I must have been a fool to think I could run 26.2 miles. Some days I just didn't have it. But I kept on going. On one very hot day, I did a fourteen miler and ran out of water at about ten miles. I trudged along to finish, figuring I would get some water at the grocery store where I had parked my car. I ended up collapsing in the grocery store and an ambulance whisked me away to the ER with a bad case of dehydration. But I didn't miss my next run, or any other run after that. I stayed positive, kept telling myself that I could do it, and I am now the proud recipient of the Marine Corps Marathon medal. At the age of thirteen, I was too fat, too slow, too negative, and certain that I couldn't run six hundred yards. At the age of fifty-nine, after surviving major depression, I completed 46,112 yards just because I told myself that I could do it. What was once considered impossible had become possible. I ran over six hundred miles to get myself ready for the marathon. The things that made it possible were positive thoughts, gratitude, saying thank you, singing songs to myself, putting one foot in front of the other, and running even when I didn't feel like it.

Chapter Twenty
Happy Endings

Through my involvement in NAMI, I was invited to attend the graduation ceremony of The RESPECT Institute. This is a three-and-a-half-day program designed to provide twelve individuals the skills and coaching necessary to transform their mental illness, treatment, and recovery experiences into educational and inspirational presentations. The RESPECT Institute helps participants organize, construct, and customize their personal stories so they can be delivered in diverse venues, like legislative meetings, employee orientations, university classrooms, civic meetings, and continuing education programs. The RESPECT Institute empowers consumers by acknowledging, honoring, and valuing their personal experiences and insights. Through this recognition and acceptance, individuals reclaim their sense of self and join an army of individuals educating their community and eliminating stigma. I was so moved by the presentations that I decided to learn more about The RESPECT Institute. Through my research, I discovered the Georgia Mental Health Consumer Network (GMHCN), a nonprofit corporation founded in 1991 by consumers of state services for mental health, developmental disabilities, and addictive diseases. One of the major initiatives of GMHCN is the Certified Peer Specialist (CPS) Project.

According to www.gmhcn.org, in December of 2001, approximately thirty-five present and former mental health consumers completed their training and examination to become Georgia's first class of Certified Peer Specialists. CPSs are responsible for the implementation of peer support services, which are Medicaid-reimbursable under Georgia's Rehab Option. They also serve on Assertive Community Treatment teams (ACT), as Community Support Individuals (CSI), and in a variety of other services designed to assist the peers they are partnered with in reaching the goals they wish to accomplish in their personal recovery journeys.

A natural outgrowth of the 1999 Surgeon General's Report on Mental Health has been the realization of the value of peer-to-peer support in the acquisition of real recovery. Certified Peer Specialists provide hope and role models that present the possibility to every peer they are partnered with. As paid employees of our public and private mental health providers, CPSs neatly transition ownership of the program into the hands of their peers.

Certified Peer Specialists work from the perspective of "having been there." Through their lived experience with recovery, they lend unique insight into mental illness and what makes recovery possible. The training and certification process prepares CPSs to promote hope, personal responsibility, empowerment, education, and self-determination in the communities in which they serve. Certified Peer Specialists are part of the shift that is taking place in the Georgia Mental Health System from one that focuses on the individual's illness to one that focuses on the individual's strength. Recovery is no longer only about what clinicians do to consumers. It has become, with the assistance of CPSs, what peers do for themselves and each other. CPSs are trained to assist their peers in skill building, goal setting, problem solving, conducting Recovery Dialogues, setting up and sustaining mutual self-help groups, and in helping their peers build their own self-directed recovery tools, including the Wellness Recovery Action Plan (WRAP). A critical role is supporting peers in developing an Individual Recovery and Resiliency Plan (IRRP) that has their recovery goals and specific steps to obtain to reach those goals. Further requirements of certification include understanding the structure of the Georgia mental health system, client rights, cultural competency, confidentiality, and the documentation require-ments for progress notes that are monitored by APS Healthcare.

I decided that I wanted to become a CPS so that I could support others in their recovery. I was already facilitating a support group for NAMI, so it seemed only natural. At the time, I was selling used cars for a living and I was looking for something more meaningful. I took the two-week-long CPS class and passed the certification examination on my first attempt. A short time later, I visited the Peer Support, Wellness, and Respite Center (PSWRC) in Bartow County. This is one of five centers in Georgia which are operated under the CPS project. I met some of the CPS staff members and observed activities in the center. I got a chance to meet some of the peers who participated in the activities, and I found it easy for me to connect with them. I decided that being a CPS was in my future, so I interviewed and was hired for a position. Working as a CPS provided me with an amazing sense of joy and gratitude. I witnessed miracles right before my eyes as peers grew in their recovery. In a brief twenty-minute phone conversation on the warm line (similar to a hot line but meant for callers who are not in crisis), peers were so thankful to have a friend to talk to, someone who understood and could support them. I was putting my illness, addiction, and recovery to good use. Since I have touched the darkness of mental illness and was able to find the light, I was able to empathize with my peers who were struggling, support them in their own efforts to find the light, to always be their source of light, and their beacon of hope.

I worked as a CPS for over a year as a part-time employee. I started working two other part-time jobs but was unable to manage the changing shifts and schedules. A few months later, I happened to see a job advertisement for an affiliate coordinator with an unidentified mental health organization. I decided to apply and when I was called for a phone interview, I was asked if I knew who the organization was. I told her that I did not and she told me it was NAMI Georgia. Well, my résumé was full of references to NAMI-related activities. I interviewed for the job at the end of the week and, at the end of the interview, I asked, "When would you like me to start?" I was offered the position and worked at NAMI Georgia for over a year and a half supporting the affiliates around the state. I began to facilitate support groups, conduct classes, and I am now a NAMI State Trainer for the Connection Recovery Support Group. I decided to leave my NAMI Georgia position to be able to do some part-time work at home, to slow down the pace of life for my own self-care. This also gives me more flexibility to be available to support my father-in-law when he has doctor appointments and needs to go grocery shopping.

When Aline was in college, she and her roommates thought it would be a good idea to get a dog. They adopted a little basset/beagle mix named Celia. She was kind of funny-looking with short legs, big paws, and floppy ears. She looked and sounded like a hound dog, but she was long and low to the ground. My daughter and her roommates had busy student schedules, so poor

Celia was left alone for long periods of time. Like most dogs with time on their hands, Celia tended to get into trouble. She would chew up shoes and other items that she could get her teeth on, including a box of chocolate. Fortunately, the chocolate did not make her sick, but it was clear that Celia was not going to work out. I decided to adopt Celia and bring her home to Georgia. Since I was working from home, I would be with her quite a bit and could keep her out of trouble. So, one snowy December night, Hilary and I drove to St. Louis to pick up Celia. My first thought about Celia was that she was a pain in the butt. Hilary and I wanted to watch an intense slasher/thriller movie called *Identity* with John Cusack. Ten strangers are stranded at a desolate Nevada motel during a nasty rainstorm. They become acquainted with each other when they realize that they're being killed off one by one. The movie has a lot of twists and turns, and it requires your full attention. But little Celia wanted to go outside and explore every fifteen minutes or so. She would look at me and wiggle her butt, walk backward, and stare at me until I would take her out in the cold, St. Louis winter. She didn't always have to go, but she enjoyed walking around and sniffing at the snow. This is how I spent my first afternoon with Celia.

We drove home to Georgia and Celia slept the whole way. Once we got home, I began life as a dog owner. Needless to say, Celia became my dog since I was home all the time. I would take her for walks in the woods, drive her to other places where we could go for walks, take her to school to pick up the kids, and just hang out together. She may be the only dog in the world who got her own roast-beef sandwich. I fed it to her at school while waiting to pick up the kids. From that point on, she loved going to drive-through windows, but she was confused when I would go to the bank and there would be no food for her.

When Celia was fourteen, she suddenly became ill. I had an appointment to take her to the veterinarian to see if she was having any ill effects from medication, but I had no idea that on Saturday, she would not be coming home. She was listless and obviously not doing well, but I didn't expect to hear that she was severely anemic due to internal bleeding. After her examination, the veterinarian told me my options, but she felt that, if Celia was her dog, she would put her down. Surgery was possible but risky and, at her age, she probably wouldn't do well. I agreed with her and I had to let her go. I sobbed and kept repeating how sorry I was, but Celia just lay there flat on her tummy. I knew it was time. But I felt like a little boy who was losing his faithful furry companion.

The next several weeks were terribly hard on me. I missed Celia so much. I was still singing songs to her as if she was still here with me. I was struggling with my attitude and motivation. My heart was in pain. I started feeling like I wanted another dog, but I didn't feel ready for the responsibility. Somehow, I didn't think Celia would understand either. But, in 2018, when I left my job, I felt like I was ready. Since I was going to be home a lot, I felt like the time was right for me to have a dog. Ironically, my daughter Hilary and her husband Ryan would be visiting us that week and they kept nudging me about looking for a dog. They convinced me to go to the Humane Society and look at the dogs. I didn't see one that I was really excited about, but we decided to go back the next day. Plus, Lauren couldn't come with us and I wouldn't make a decision without her. So, the next day, we all went to see the dogs again. This time, there was a dog who wasn't there the day before. She had coloring similar to Celia's but she was bigger and taller. She looked like she was part shepherd and part pit, perhaps other things too. She had these cute light-brown spots above her eyes. She looked at us through the glass door and stared. Her name was Blue and, since Blue is the color of our alma mater (maize and blue), it seemed like a good fit. We decided to visit with her and we took her home.

Blue has become my new best friend. She sleeps most of the day, but she enjoys going with me to the dog park. She has quite a dominating streak in her. When I work on my computer or cell phone and she feels like it's her turn for attention, she lets me know in no uncertain terms. She jumps up on me or sits on me and insists that I stop what I am doing and pet her. Of course, I don't mind this a bit. She can be a nuisance with her squeaky toys and her burrowing under our covers at night. And she barks like crazy whenever she sees a dog outside. She doesn't care much for leashes. It feels so good to have a doggie again and to be her little boy. I think Celia approves and is happy that I am happy.

I am certain that my "re-jew-venation" has had a significantly positive impact on my life. I have been reading texts about Jewish ethics, studying with our rabbi, and have volunteered to be a member of our synagogue executive board. My time with the rabbi has been such a joy for me and is a great example of how far I have come. I used to think that a rabbi was above me in stature. I had no business talking with a rabbi, let alone asking him questions to show how ignorant I am. I would never have taken a class with a rabbi, since I knew so little about the Torah and our history. Well, shouldn't that make me the perfect candidate to take a class with the rabbi? I now ask questions freely and often find that my insights are valuable to the class. I also find that there is not always one answer and sometimes even the rabbi doesn't know an answer. My fear of disclosing my ignorance has been replaced with a thirst for knowledge and a desire to understand. I am no longer the child who is afraid to ask.

Life has become more joyous than ever. I no longer have a house to worry about. My children are happy and doing well. I have three wonderful and amazing grandchildren. My wife and I still love each other after these long and often trying years. I have retired and the financial future looks good. I am reconnecting with my synagogue and am rekindling my faith. Feelings of gratitude are slowly replacing feelings of guilt, shame, envy, and doubt. Life is not perfect. It doesn't work that way. There will be more hard times ahead. There will be bad days. There will be sadness and loss. We lost my father-in-law, Harvey, one of my supporters and best friends during the writing of this book. And, someday, I will have to deal with my own mortality and fear of death. But for now, I am grateful for all of my gifts, talents, and even my terrible puns. I am grateful for once being at rock bottom so I can truly appreciate the good things in life. I am grateful for my feelings of depression so I can truly appreciate happiness. I am grateful for feeling totally alone so I can truly empathize with others who feel that way. And I am grateful to God, who has granted me this brief moment in time called life so I can truly experience the miracles around me and know that my family will continue to prosper long after I am gone.

Chapter Twenty-One
What Can Be Done?

There was very little information research done regarding cybersex addiction or internet infidelity in the 1990s. With the advent of technology, pornographic images, sexting, and other forms of sexual content are now in the palms of one's hand. Sexual addiction is on the rise and is impacting even teens and young adults. Based on research and studies performed by Dr. Kimberly Young, we know a great deal more about the subject of cybersex and its impact on our society.

There are many names used to describe cybersex. It can be referred to as cyber affairs, cyber cheating, online affairs, internet affairs, or internet infidelity. According to Dr. Young, it is "a romantic affair involving intimate or sexually explicit communication between two people, one of whom is married or in a committed relationship, which is conducted primarily in cyberspace over the internet." The *Diagnostic and Statistical Manual of Mental Disorders*, fifth edition: DSM-5, by American Psychiatric Association (May 27, 2013), does not list sex addiction as a diagnosable condition yet, but research indicates that there is a clear prevalence of adverse sexual behavior that is similar in development to a "chemical" addiction.

Robert Gray

Such online affairs have become more prevalent in recent years. One no longer has to set up clandestine meetings and run the risk of getting caught. Online meetings can occur in the comfort and safety of one's own home. The ease of finding partners and the practically twenty-four/seven availability for meetings to occur has made the internet a popular choice for those looking for cybersex.

When I began using the internet for sex, I didn't regard it as cheating or infidelity. It was fun and exciting and, like any addiction, it gave me an escape from my real-world issues. Dr. Young's research has found that those involved in internet infidelity undergo personality changes and are able to rationalize that an online affair is not cheating. It is often viewed as "harmless flirtation" without any "physical touching," without recognition of the potential destructive consequences.

In actuality, online affairs are a form of emotional infidelity. As with me, online affairs often begin in cyberspace but then may progress to email contact, telephone calls, US mail, and eventually personal contact. In fact, studies have shown that there are connections between internet affairs and sexual affairs.

According to research cited by Dr. Young in *Sexting, Snapchat, and Other Forms of Internet Infidelity* (Founder, Center for Internet Addiction):

- According to statistics, 50 percent of people

who engage in internet chats have made phone contact with someone they chatted with online.

- One study found that 30 percent of cyber affairs escalate from e-mail to telephone calls to personal contact.
- Another study found that 31 percent of people had an online conversation that eventually led to real-time sex.
- Internet infidelity has resulted in an increase in the number of divorces and separations.

We are so dependent on our technology and devices in both our professional and private lives that is it extremely difficult to see the symptoms of an online affair. There were times back in the 1990s when I would be carrying on a conversation on my laptop with an online partner while my children were in the room with me. They would be doing their homework or watching TV with me without a single thought as to what I was doing. Nowadays, the cell phone and various apps make it even easier to communicate without being suspected. According to Dr. Young, there are behavioral changes to look for if one suspects internet infidelity. These behavioral changes may include:

- Change in sleep patterns—I would often go to bed at 2:00 a.m. after several hours of internet time. My alarm would go off at 6:30 a.m. so I could help get my kids off to school and get to work. I would get through the day on adrenalin and somehow manage to function at a fairly high level.

- A demand for privacy—I did all I could to keep my online behavior a secret. My computer was in the basement for some time, so I was often alone. Eventually, I moved to a laptop so I could be online anywhere in the house. Even if my wife or children were nearby, I would keep my screen hidden from view. At work, I would look for vacant conference rooms, where I would pretend that I needed a quiet space to work. From there, I would sometimes make or receive phone calls.

- Household chores ignored—I did my best to keep up with the dishes and the laundry as well as carpooling for the kids. Working at home made this easier since I had more hours in the day to get things done, even while working or playing in cyberspace. However, some of the larger chores such as home maintenance would likely be ignored because they took too much time or cost too much money.

- Evidence of lying—In the 1990s, cell phone and landline bills contained details of every call. It was imperative for me to get these bills from the mailbox and make sure that they were kept from my wife. I couldn't run the risk of being found out and having to make up some lie about the calls. I kept all of the credit card bills from being found as well since I was racking up hundreds of dollars per month on internet charges. When I had a secret post office box, I never kept the key on my key ring for fear of having to explain it. If I was traveling on business and incurred telephone charges in my hotel, I would pay them in cash so they would not appear on the company credit card statement. I also used prepaid long-distance cards to enable me to make calls without receiving a bill. I did whatever I had to do to hide the evidence of my shameful escapades. I even lied to my online partners. If I didn't want them to know I was online, I would use a different screen name so even they couldn't catch me.

- Loss of interest in sex—Since I was getting to bed at such late hours, this was not much of an issue. Early on, I didn't lose interest in sex. However, my fantasy thoughts would sometimes interfere with the pleasure of the physical act of making love. I would sometimes try to incorporate some of these fantasies by trying things I had done in cyberspace, most notably, on our twentieth wedding anniversary that we spent in a romantic spot on the Pacific Coast. I didn't respond the way I expected to and I lay awake for a couple of hours listening to the waves and wondering what was wrong with me. This was only about two months prior to my physical encounter with my cyber partner.

- Declining investment in the relationship—
Over time, the cyber relationship began to
overtake the real world one. Thoughts,
feelings, and energy became focused on the
fantasy. Doing things with the family become
less interesting and important. The possibilities
of running away to live in the fantasy world
began to enter my mind, although I never
actually believed I would ever leave my family.
I became a stranger to my wife and children.

Motivations to engage in cybersex are much the
same as for other addictions such as drugs, alcohol,
or gambling. Often, there is a need to avoid real-
life issues and stresses and to make oneself numb.
There is a sense of euphoria that accompanies the
pleasurable aspect of the addiction. However, this
sense of pleasure is often followed by pain, guilt,
and remorse. The addict promises himself that he
will change his behavior but he is often
unsuccessful. The grip of the addiction is too tight.

Dr. Young cites the following motivations in her
book *Sexting, Snapchat, and Other Forms of Online
Porn Addiction and Internet Infidelity* (Center for
Internet Addiction, March 2, 2014):

- Free from STDs—This was never an issue for
me at first, since I had no intention of physical
contact. Cybersex enables "no-risk" sex.
However, once the idea of physical contact
became real, I became very worried about

AIDS. My fear of disease was most likely a factor in my inability to forgive myself. I was afraid that I would pass on a disease to my family.

- Empowerment—In the real world, I rarely had conversations about sex. I was always too shy to talk about it. On the internet, I became a different person. I could say whatever I wanted and do whatever I could imagine. I could have different types of relationships and partners. If I wanted to experiment, I could always find new and willing partners. The shyness was gone.

- Intensifies self-stimulation and masturbation—Being online provided me a new and unique experience each time. The possibilities of partners and fantasy scenarios were practically endless. As Forrest Gump said, "You never know what you're gonna get." I had experience with masturbating with fantasies in my head, but the internet was even more stimulating since I could also imagine, or hear, a partner living in my fantasy.

- Escape from stress and tension—Many addicts use their drug of choice as a way to avoid the pressures of life. I was in a job that I didn't like, I felt incompetent at work, and my wife and I were raising four children—three of whom were triplets. Since my schedule was more flexible and I worked at home some of the time, I was usually the parent who dealt with after-school activities and carpooling to religious school. At times, I felt a great deal of stress and I actually enjoyed being out of town on business, even before my addictive behavior began. Eventually, the euphoria of cybersex provided me with an escape from my real-life stress.

- Normalizes sexual fantasies—As I have mentioned, sex was not talked about in my home as a child and, even as an adult, it was not discussed. My first impression of sex was that it was a bad thing, and I forgave my parents for doing it twice. I was never told that masturbation was bad, but it was also something I never disclosed to anyone. My first experience with sexual intercourse was on my wedding night and, even then, I wasn't sure I knew how to do it. Online sex provided me a place to be open about sex and to say anything I want.

- Provides approval and affirmation—I was not usually happy with my physical appearance. As a child, I felt judged because I was usually overweight. I was never a cool kid. As an adult, my weight was usually an issue as well. The online world makes this a nonissue. I would tell people anything I wanted to about my appearance, and they would never disapprove.

- Alleviates performance anxiety—Performance anxiety was never a big issue for me. However, I often felt like I had so little experience and didn't really know enough. My wife and I did not have conversations about this subject and, of course, I never expressed my feelings of possible inadequacy. In some ways, cyber relationships made me more confident because my partners provided me positive messages.

- Coping with childhood abuse—I was most certainly not raised in an abusive household. My childhood environment was impacted by the Holocaust experiences of my parents and other relatives. There was little conversation, few displays of affection, and few outward displays of happiness. I don't know how this has impacted me with respect to sexual behavior and compulsions, but I have to believe that I paid an emotional price.

If you are struggling with internet infidelity or cybersex issues and want to do what it takes to prevent it, Dr. Young recommends the following (*Sexting, Snapchat, and Other Forms of Online Porn Addiction and Internet Infidelity*, Kindle Edition, Center for Internet Addiction, March 2, 2014):

- **Maintain appropriate walls and windows.**
  Avoid using the internet in areas where you can hide out. Do not hang out in places where you can maintain secrecy. Do not let your screen be hidden.
- **Recognize that work can be a danger zone.**
  Many online affairs can begin in the workplace.

Do not always go to lunch or take breaks with the same person.

- **Avoid emotional intimacy with attractive alternatives to your committed relationship.**
Stay away from possibly dangerous situations with an attractive coworker.

- **Protect your marriage by discussing relationship issues at home.**
Be open with your partner about feelings and emotions. Communication is the key to resolving issues.

- **Keep old flames from reigniting.**
Social media makes it easy to track down people from your past. Keep your distance and avoid complications.

- **Don't go over the line when online with internet friends.**
Over time, online relationships can grow as people get to know each other. This can lead to real friendships and the need for emotional support. Keep your boundaries and don't stray from your real world.

- **Make sure your social network is supportive of your marriage.**
Keep your marriage and family life in the forefront and share information with your online friends so that they know, understand, and support your marital relationship.

The good news is that sex addiction can be treated by a mental health professional, like a psychologist or licensed social worker. They will help you address some of the underlying factors that are maintaining your addiction and teach you to find healthy ways to cope with your thoughts, feelings, and behaviors.

According to Dr. Robert Weiss and Dr. Jennifer Schneider, cybersex addiction can be treated successfully (*Always Turned On: Sex Addiction in the Digital Age*, Gentle Path Press, February 17, 2015). However, recovery is not as simple as saying, "I'll never do that again." Behavior change can and does occur, but recovery usually requires hard work and outside assistance. Drs. Weiss and Schneider recommend the following actions:

- Find a professional therapist trained in the treatment of addiction AND sexual disorders.
- Find a support group.
- Find an accountability partner.
- Throw out all physical material related to the problem.
- "Clean" digital devices while being monitored by the accountability partner.
- Cancel any memberships to websites, apps, and brick-and-mortar stores that service the problematic behavior.
- Stay away from "gray-area" activities.
- Orient home and work computers in a public-facing direction.
- Display inspirational photos.
- Install filtering/accountability software on digital devices.

Epilogue

When I first thought about writing this book, I felt that it would be helpful for people who are susceptible to internet infidelity or cybersex addiction. I hoped that it would provide some hope for those struggling with similar issues. But writing the book was instrumental for me to put the pieces together. I was able to connect my remembrances of the past as if I were doing a jigsaw puzzle. One piece at a time, the puzzle of my life was laid out before me and things began to make sense to me.

The most important learning for me was that there were so many times when I should have asked for help, admitted my weaknesses, and accepted my vulnerabilities. There were so many opportunities to realize that I didn't have to do it alone. I didn't have to act brave and hide behind my mask. When I needed help, all I had to do was ask.

If you are like I was, please don't make yourself go it alone. Speak up. Ask. Come out from the shadows of your insecurities. Don't be the fifth child who is afraid to ask. There is an old joke about how many Jewish mothers does it take to screw in a lightbulb, and the answer is none, they'd rather sit in the dark. Believe me when I tell you

Robert Gray

that it is much better to bask in the light, even if
you have to ask someone to help you screw in the
lightbulb. Be well!

Acknowledgments

I would like to thank my wife Lauren and my children Aline, Hilary, Michael, and Eric for helping me throughout the long process of creating this book. I would also like to thank the many friends and peers who have urged me to tell my story for the benefit of others. Thank you to Mountain Arbor Press for their professional publishing services to make this book a reality.

About the Author

Robert Gray was born in Detroit, Michigan, in 1954. His parents were Holocaust survivors from Hungary. He spent most of his career in various quality assurance positions until 2015 when he became a Certified Peer Specialist and later worked for the National Alliance on Mental Illness,

Robert and his doggie, Blue

for whom he is now a volunteer peer mentor and support group facilitator. Robert is a grateful husband, father, and grandfather and resides in Roswell, Georgia. His hobbies include music, thinking of clever puns, and loving his dog, Blue.

You may contact Robert at
info@releasingtheboundsofshame.com.